DINOSAURS
GREAT and SMALL

DINOSAURS GREAT and SMALL

A Supplement to
Childcraft—The How and Why Library

World Book, Inc.
a Scott Fetzer company
Chicago
www.worldbook.com

Staff

Executive Committee

President
Jim O'Rourke
Vice President, Finance
Donald D. Keller
Vice President and Editor in Chief
Paul A. Kobasa
Vice President, Technology
Sanjay Gupta
Vice President, Marketing
Jean Lin
Director, International Sales
Kristin Norell
Director, Human Resources
Bev Ecker

Editorial

Manager, Annuals/Series Nonfiction
Christine Sullivan
Editor, Annuals/Series Nonfiction
Kendra Muntz
Manager, Indexing Services
David Pofelski
Manager, Contracts & Compliance (Rights & Permissions)
Loranne K. Shields
Administrative Assistant
Ethel Matthews

Editorial Administration

Senior Manager, Publishing Operations
Timothy Falk

Production

Manufacturing Manager
Sandra Johnson
Production/Technology Manager
Anne Fritzinger
Proofreader
Nathalie Strassheim

Graphics and Design

Senior Art Director
Tom Evans
Senior Designer
Don Di Sante

Marketing

Director, Direct Marketing
Mark R. Willy
Marketing Analyst
Zofia Kulik

For information about other World Book publications, visit our website at www.worldbook.com or call 1-800-WORLDBK (967-5325). For information about sales to schools and libraries, call 1-800-975-3250 (United States) or 1-800-837-5365 (Canada).

© 2016 World Book, Inc. All rights reserved. This volume may not be reproduced in whole or in part in any form without prior written permission from the publisher.

© 2013, 2006 Amber Books Ltd., London

CHILDCRAFT, CHILDCRAFT—THE HOW AND WHY LIBRARY, and the GLOBE DEVICE are registered trademarks or trademarks of World Book, Inc.

World Book, Inc.
180 N. LaSalle St., Suite 900
Chicago, IL 60601
U.S.A.

Childcraft Annual—Dinosaurs Great and Small
ISBN:
978-0-7166-0634-5

Printed in China by Shenzhen Donnelley Printing Co., Ltd., Guangdong Province
1st printing December 2015

Library of Congress Cataloging-in-Publication Data

Dinosaurs great and small: a supplement to Childcraft, the how and why library.
    pages cm
  Summary: "An introduction to various types of dinosaurs: Giant sauropods, large theropods, small theropods, and armored and duckbilled dinosaurs. Features include an original drawing of each dinosaur, fun facts, and a list of additional resources"-- Provided by publisher.
  Includes index.
  ISBN 978-0-7166-0634-5
  1. Dinosaurs--Juvenile literature. I. World Book, Inc.
  QE861.5.D5644 2016
  567.91--dc23
                                            2015035912

Contents

Introduction 8

GIANT DINOSAURS—The Sauropods 10

ARMORED DINOSAURS—The Ornithischians 46

FIERCE DINOSAURS—The Large Theropods 82

BIRDLIKE DINOSAURS—Small Theropods and
    Prehistoric Birds 116

Where to Find Dinosaurs and Additional Resources 150

Index 157

Acknowledgments

The publishers of *Childcraft—The How and Why Library* gratefully acknowledge the courtesy of the following individuals and agencies for illustrations in this volume. When all the illustrations for a sequence of pages are from a single source, the inclusive page numbers are given. Credits should be read left to right, top to bottom, on their respective pages. All illustrations are the exclusive property of World Book, Inc. unless otherwise noted.

Covers

Aristocrat, Discovery, and Standard Bindings: Amber Books and WORLD BOOK (Ian Jackson, The Art Agency)

Heritage Binding: Don Di Sante; © Louie Psihoyos, Science Faction/SuperStock; © Marcio Silva, iStockphoto; © Science Faction/SuperStock; © Chris Howes, Wild Places Photography/Alamy Images

Rainbow Binding: © Robert Miramontes, iStockphoto; © Phil Degginger, Alamy Images

Illustrations

Amber Books and WORLD BOOK (Ian Jackson, The Art Agency)

Photographs and maps

- 2: © IrinaK, Shutterstock
- 9: WORLD BOOK maps
- 10: Don Di Sante
- 11: © Science Faction/SuperStock
- 13: © Jeff Morgan 03, Alamy
- 15: © Chris Howes, Wild Places Photography/Alamy Images
- 22: © Phil Degginger, Alamy Images
- 34: © Bjanka Kadic, Alamy Images
- 45: © Mark Garlick, Photo Researchers
- 46: Don Di Sante
- 47: © Andy Crawford, Dorling Kindersley
- 49: © amberstock, Alamy
- 51: © The Natural History Museum/The Image Works
- 58: © July Flower, Shutterstock
- 65: © Oleksiy Maksymenko, All Canada Photos/SuperStock
- 73: © Lynton Gardiner, American Museum of Natural History/Dorling Kindersley
- 81: © Science Faction/SuperStock
- 82: Don Di Sante
- 83: © Andy Crawford, Dorling Kindersley
- 85: © Hans Winke, Alamy
- 87: © Louie Psihoyos, Corbis
- 93: © Science Faction/SuperStock
- 103: © Walter Geiersperger, Corbis
- 115: © Science Faction/SuperStock
- 116: © Jason Edwards, National Geographic Stock
- 117: © Andy Crawford, Dorling Kindersley
- 119: © blickwinkel, Alamy
- 120: © O. Louis Mazzatenta, National Geographic Stock
- 139: © incamerastock/Alamy Images
- 140: © O. Louis Mazzatenta, National Geographic Stock
- 149: © Dave Watts, Alamy Images
- 150: © Kayte Deioma, ZUMAPress/Alamy Images
- 151: Don Di Sante
- 152: © Richard Cummins, Corbis
- 153: © Richard T. Nowitz, Corbis
- 154: © Flirt/SuperStock
- 155: © Travelscape Images/Alamy Images

Preface

The dinosaurs died out millions of years ago, but they have fascinated people ever since they were first described in the early 1800's. The name dinosaur comes from the term Dinosauria, which means *terribly great lizards*. But dinosaurs were not lizards. They were only distantly related to them, and most dinosaurs were not very terrible.

Some of the best-known dinosaurs were terrifying, however. Many were GIANT, such as the sauropods (*SAWR uh PAHDZ*). These dinosaurs towered above and weighed more than any other animal ever to live on land. The largest dinosaurs may have grown as long as 130 feet (40 meters) and weighed as much as 85 tons (77 metric tons). Such giants would have been more than 10 times as heavy as a full-grown elephant.

Ornithischians were ARMORED dinosaurs that carried their own protective armor with them in the form of plates and horns. They needed protection given the kinds of dangerous dinosaurs they lived among.

Size was not the only characteristic that made some dinosaurs terrifying, however. Of the theropods, some were huge—for example, Tyrannosaurus rex was as long as 40 feet (12.3 meters). Other theropods were more the size of an ostrich, but they were still FIERCE and deadly meat-eaters. The smallest kinds—including some of the smaller theropods—were BIRDLIKE approximately, the size of a chicken.

This book covers all four of these types of dinosaurs, which include many of the ones people love best.

Introduction

We are fascinated by the dinosaurs and the time in which they lived. Earth went through great changes during the Age of Dinosaurs.

Earth has an outer shell made up of about 30 rigid pieces called tectonic plates. The plates move about on a layer of rock that is so hot it flows, even though it remains solid. The plates are moving very slowly, at speeds up to about 4 inches (10 centimeters) per year.

Earth's plates have been moving about for hundreds of millions of years. So, in spite of their very low speeds, some of them have moved vast distances. Some of these plates are gigantic. For instance, most of the Pacific Ocean covers a single plate.

At the start of the Age of the Dinosaurs, a huge supercontinent called Pangaea (pan-JEE-uh) was surrounded by a great ocean. Pangaea broke apart over millions of years, and the continents began to drift toward the positions they occupy today.

There also were great changes in plants and animals. Early in the Age of Dinosaurs,

Dinosaurs first appeared during the Triassic Period. They became the largest, most successful land animals early in the Jurassic Period. The dinosaurs died out at the end of the Cretaceous Period. Together, these three periods make up the Mesozoic Era, the Age of Dinosaurs.

The Age of Dinosaurs

Period	Triassic	Jurassic	Cretaceous
Began	252 million years ago	201 million years ago	145 million years ago
Ended	201 million years ago	145 million years ago	66 million years ago
Major Events	Dinosaurs first appeared but did not become common until the end of this period.	Dinosaurs became the largest animals everywhere on land, reaching their greatest size.	A mass extinction at the end of this period killed off all the dinosaurs except some birds.

such seed plants as conifers, cycads, and ginkgoes were common.

The first true mammals appeared, and crocodilians, frogs, insects, and lizards flourished. Flying reptiles called pterosaurs *(TEHR-uh-sawrz)* filled the skies.

Plesiosaurs *(PLEE-see-uh-sawrz)* and other marine reptiles ruled the oceans. Later, flowering plants appeared and began to replace seed plants in some areas, helping insects and mammals to thrive. Birds arose from small meat-eating dinosaurs and soon spread around the world. The first snakes appeared, along with modern bony fish.

200 million years ago

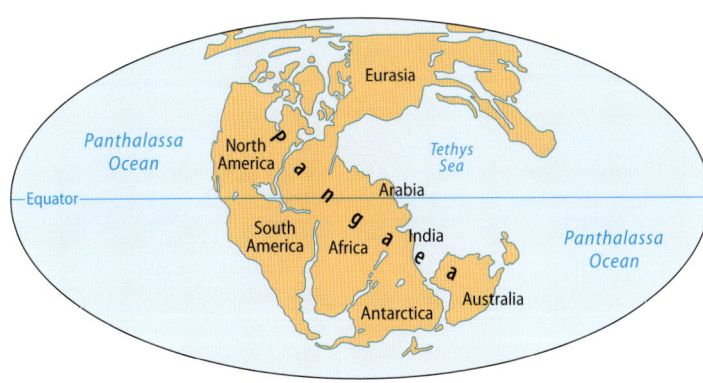

About 200 million years ago *(above)* a supercontinent that scientists call Pangaea was surrounded by a vast ocean. Pangaea broke up into separate continents during the Age of Dinosaurs. By 100 million years ago *(below)*, the continents had begun to drift toward the positions they occupy today.

100 million years ago

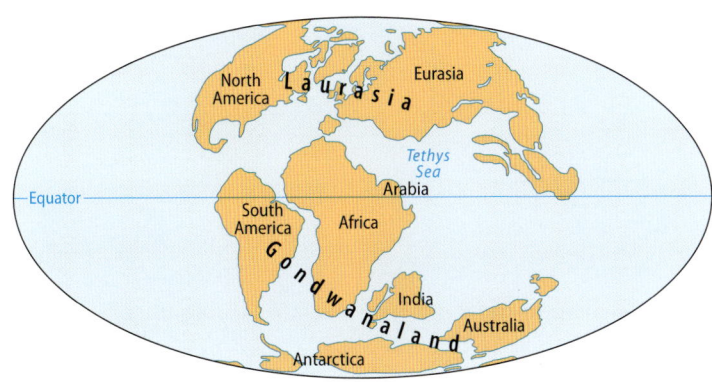

GIANT DINOSAURS

The Sauropods

Imagine standing in a forest 100 million years ago as a mighty dinosaur tears away great mouthfuls of leaves from branches high up in a tree. You are watching a sauropod *(SAWR-uh-PAHD)*, the largest of all the dinosaurs. This giant is far larger than any land animal alive today. In fact, some sauropods were the largest animals ever to live on land, reaching up to 130 feet (40 meters) long and weighing up to 85 tons (77 metric tons)!

Sauropods ate huge amounts of plants every day. Their long necks allowed them to graze on ferns and shrubs near the ground or to reach leaves on the tallest trees. Sauropods also had a small head, a long tail, and a huge, deep chest and stomach. Their whiplike tail and huge body helped to protect them from attackers. Some sauropods traveled in large herds for

Paleontologist Fernando Novas of Argentina stands next to a fossil thighbone of the giant sauropod Antarctosaurus *(above)*. **A reconstruction of a Diplodocus skeleton** *(left)* **dominates the Central Hall of the Natural History Museum in London.**

11

protection from huge meat-eating dinosaurs that roamed the land.

How did sauropods get so big? This question fascinates scientists and the public alike. To become so large, sauropods had to overcome many challenges. From tiny hatchlings, they had to grow many thousands of times heavier in just a few decades in order to reach full size. In order to grow, a sauropod had to eat tons of food with its small head. Its heart had to be very strong to pump blood all the way up its long neck to reach its brain. By studying sauropod fossils and the places in which they lived, paleontologists (people who study animals, plants, and other things that lived in prehistoric times [more than 5,500 years ago]) learn how these huge animals overcame such challenges.

Scientists put sauropods and their ancestors into a larger group known as sauropodomorphs (SAWR-*uh*-PAHD-*uh*-*mawrphs*). The earliest sauropodomorphs, called prosauropods, appeared about 230 million years ago, in the Triassic Period. During the Age of Dinosaurs, which lasted from about 252 million to 66 million years ago, sauropods spread to nearly every area of Earth. They were especially successful during the Jurassic Period, which lasted from about 201 million to 145 million years ago. Many new species also appeared toward the end of the Cretaceous Period, which lasted from about 145 million years ago to 66 million years ago.

A life-sized model of a Brachiosaurus, from the Dan-yr-Ogof National Showcaves Centre for Wales, in the United Kingdom.

Prosauropods

The prosauropods thrived at the beginning of the Age of Dinosaurs. They were the first dinosaurs to reach enormous sizes. There were many different kinds of prosauropods. Some were small, while others weighed more than a fully grown elephant.

The earliest prosauropods lived about 230 million years ago, in the middle of the Triassic Period. They were small animals that weighed no more than about 20 to 30 pounds (9 to 14 kilograms). Most walked on their long hind legs. Later, these animals grew so large that they had to walk on all fours.

All prosauropods had sturdy bodies and long, thin necks with small heads. Many had large claws that may have been used to gather vegetation or to fight off predators. Prosauropods fed on the leaves of trees, or they ate ferns and herbs on the ground. Scientists think their teeth were used to bite off parts of plants—they were not shaped for chewing. These dinosaurs may have had a muscular stomach, much like the gizzard of a modern bird. They also swallowed stones that helped grind up plant matter into a digestible pulp.

For reasons unknown, the prosauropods died out early in the Jurassic Period, which began about 201 million years ago. However, scientists believe that certain prosauropods were the ancestors of sauropods. Along with other dinosaurs, these giants spread throughout the world.

Large prosauropods walked on all fours *(below)*, but most could stand up on their rear legs to reach food high in the trees *(left)*.

Coloradisaurus

(kol-oh-RAHD-uh-SAWR-us)
Coloradisaurus walked on four legs but stood on its rear legs to feed on leaves from high branches. It may have used its clawed upper limbs to defend itself.

FUN FACT
The name "Euskelosaurus" means "good leg lizard." At 33 feet (10 meters) long, it was one of the largest dinosaurs at the time.

Euskelosaurus

(yoo-skel-o-SAWR-us)
Euskelosaurus ate huge amounts of *foliage* (leaves and stems) and could strip a whole area of its plant life. It was the first dinosaur discovered in Africa, where its fossils were found in 1863.

Melanorosaurus

(muh-LAN-or-o-SAWR-us)
Melanorosaurus had a large body and sturdy limbs. It had spoon-shaped teeth that were ideal for raking leaves off branches.

Riojasaurus
(ree-OH-ha-SAWR-us)
A fully grown Riojasaurus could weigh up to 1,500 pounds (680 kilograms). Because it was so heavy, it could not stand on its back legs to feed, as other prosauropods did.

FUN FACT
Dozens of Plateosaurus skeletons have been discovered. Because of this, scientists have learned a lot about their life history.

Plateosaurus
(PLATE-ee-o-SAWR-us)
Plateosaurus had a long neck and tail, features that were important for later sauropods. It had a large claw on its thumb to grab branches and pull them to its mouth.

17

UP CLOSE

Mussaurus (moo-SAWR-us)

lived in what is now South America about 220 million years ago. The first Mussaurus fossils discovered were those of babies. Mussaurus means "mouse lizard." This name refers to the dinosaur's young, which were only a bit larger than a mouse.

The discovery of Mussaurus young helped scientists learn how the dinosaurs reproduced and cared for their young. Mussaurus lived in groups of both adults and young. This arrangement would have provided some defense from meat-eating dinosaurs.

FACT O SAUR

Scientists think that many Mussaurus young were likely eaten before they reached adulthood.

Mussaurus adults were about 10 feet (3 meters) long, including the tail.

These relatively small prosauropods ate mostly low-growing ferns and other soft plants, which they bit off with their long, slender teeth.

Mussaurus had strong legs and could probably move quickly, running on all four limbs.

18

Thecodontosaurus
(THEE-co-dont-oh-SAWR-us)
Thecodontosaurus was particularly quick because of its small size—it grew to only about 8 feet (2.5 meters) long. When threatened, it stood up and sprinted away.

Ammosaurus
(am-o-SAWR-us)
Ammosaurus lived about 190 million years ago in what is now North America. A fossil Ammosaurus was found with the bones of another smaller dinosaur in its stomach area. Scientists think this prosauropod may have eaten both animals and plants.

Anchisaurus

(an-key-SAWR-us)

A small dinosaur, Anchisaurus was about 7 feet (2 meters) in length. Like many plant-eating dinosaurs, Anchisaurus swallowed small stones that helped to grind up plant food in the dinosaur's stomach.

FUN FACT

Yunnanosaurus had up to 60 spoon-shaped teeth in its mouth. The teeth wore against each other as the dinosaur bit down, which kept the teeth sharp.

Yunnanosaurus

(YOU-nahn-o-SAWR-us)

Yunnanosaurus was well-equipped for gathering leaves from high in the trees. Its body was up to 60 feet (17 meters) long. It could stand on two legs and pull branches down with its claws.

20

Lufengosaurus *(loo-feng-o-SAWR-us)*

lived in what is now China about 200 million to 180 million years ago. It is one of the best-known of all prosauropods because so many of its fossils have been found. Lufengosaurus weighed up to 1,200 pounds (500 kilograms) and reached 20 feet (6.5 meters) long.

UP CLOSE

FACT O SAUR
Like most prosauropods, Lufengosaurus had hind legs that were longer and thicker than its forelegs.

The long, slender jaws were full of small, spoon-shaped teeth, suitable for biting off leaves. These teeth could not chew food.

Lufengosaurus had powerful claws, especially on its thumbs.

Lufengosaurus broke up and ground its food with a muscular stomach, which contained stones, like the gizzards of many birds today.

21

Jurassic Sauropods

Sauropods first appeared more than 200 million years ago, but scientists do not know much about their early history. They became more common during the early part of the Jurassic Period, which lasted from about 201 million to 145 million years ago. Sauropods soon spread all over the world.

All sauropods were large, sturdy animals with legs like columns—much like elephants today. They had long, slender necks, small heads, and very long tails. They all ate plants. However, we know that not all sauropods were alike. Some could lift their necks high into the air and probably grazed on the tops of trees like giraffes. Others fed close to the ground.

Scientists have found thousands of sauropod footprints all over the world, and these show that many of these dinosaurs lived and moved in herds. In the late Jurassic Period, sauropods were among the most common dinosaurs. Many different kinds of sauropods lived alongside one another, which suggests that they ate different kinds of plants. As the Jurassic Period ended, about 145 million years ago, many of the sauropods began to die out. Scientists are not sure why many sauropods disappeared at this time.

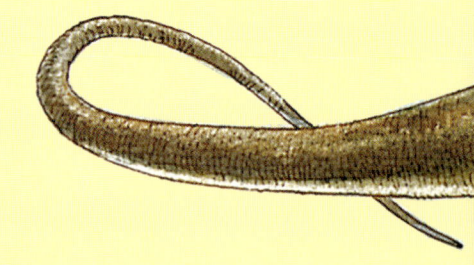

The fossilized skull of Camarasaurus *(left)*, a common sauropod dinosaur from North America, has many hollow spaces. Many sauropods had such holes, which helped to reduce the weight of the head at the end of the animal's long neck.

Kotasaurus

(KOHT-ah-SAWR-us)
Kotasaurus was an early sauropod known from fossils found in India. It has some features in common with prosauropods. It was about 30 feet (9 meters) long.

Barapasaurus

(buh-RAH-pah-SAWR-us)
Hundreds of fossils found together at a single site in India suggest that Barapasaurus lived in herds. This living arrangement provided protection from meat-eating dinosaurs.

Patagosaurus

(PAT-ah-goh-SAWR-us)
This early sauropod is known from fossils found in South America. It may be a close relative of Cetiosaurus.

FUN FACT

Scientists first discovered bones of Vulcanodon inside the gut of a large, meat-eating dinosaur. The Vulcanodon had been eaten, bones and all!

Vulcanodon
(vul-kan-oh-DON)
Vulcanodon was a mid-sized early sauropod known from fossils found in Africa. Scientists think it may represent a link between the prosauropods and the larger sauropods that appeared later.

Cetiosaurus
(SEAT-ee-oh-SAWR-us)
The name Cetiosaurus means "whale lizard." Scientists first thought that this dinosaur was a sea creature. It was later recognized as a sauropod. But it may have lived near water.

25

UP CLOSE

Brachiosaurus (brack-ee-uh-SAWR-us)

was a gigantic sauropod that looked somewhat like an enormous giraffe. It weighed up to 85 tons (77 metric tons) and stood more than 40 feet (12 meters) tall.

Brachiosaurus's head had a broad, flat snout and a large, dome-shaped ridge above the eyes. The nostrils opened from the ridge at the very top of the head, so this dinosaur did not have to stop eating to breathe.

FACT O SAUR

Brachiosaurus lived on the open plains of North America and Africa about 150 million years ago, feeding off the treetops.

Brachiosaurus's mouth was well-equipped to eat massive amounts of plants. It had up to 52 chisel-shaped teeth. The teeth were used to rake in leaves rather than for chewing.

Brachiosaurus was so tall that it could always find food high in the trees, even during *droughts* (unusually dry and rainless times). Other sauropods could not reach so high into the treetops.

Datousaurus
(dah-toe-SAWR-us)
Datousaurus had a body about 50 feet (15 meters) long, ending in a thin tail. Fossils of this creature are not found in groups, unlike those of many other sauropods. Therefore, scientists think this dinosaur may not have lived in herds.

Brontosaurus
(BRON-toh-SAWR-us)
Brontosaurus lived in western North America. People used to think it was the same animal as Apatosaurus, but scientists recently discovered that they are different dinosaurs. Its name means "thunder lizard."

FUN FACT
Different kinds of sauropods often lived in the same region. Each kind probably ate different plants, so they did not fight over food.

Lapparentosaurus
(lah-pah-rent-oh-SAWR-us)
Lapparentosaurus is a sauropod dinosaur known from only a few fossils found on the island of Madagascar. No skull has been found, so scientists are not sure what it looked like.

FUN FACT

Euhelopus was the first fossil sauropod found in China. This dinosaur was discovered there in 1929.

Euhelopus
(you-HEL-oh-pus)
The name Euhelopus means "good marsh foot." Scientists gave the dinosaur this name because they thought it lived in marshy areas.

Diplodocus (di-PLOD-o-kus)

was a huge sauropod that lived about 150 million years ago in what is now North America. Diplodocus could reach a length of 90 feet (27 meters). But it was slender in build. Diplodocus usually weighed only about 11 tons (10 metric tons), though some individuals may have grown much larger.

UP CLOSE

Diplodocus had 15 bones in its neck. These bones were hollow—if they had been solid, the dinosaur would not have been to lift its own neck.

The tail of Diplodocus had more than 80 bones. It reached about 45 feet (14 meters) long, tapering to a thin tip. Diplodocus could have swung the tail like a whip to defend itself.

Scientists believe Diplodocus usually fed close to the ground, because its neck was not very flexible.

FACT O SAUR

Diplodocus's teeth were long and thin and found only at the front of the mouth. The dinosaur tore at leaves rather than chewing them.

29

UP CLOSE

Shunosaurus (SHOO-no-SAWR-us)

lived in what is now China during the middle part of the Jurassic Period, about 170 million years ago. This plant-eating giant grew to about 33 feet (11 meters) in length and weighed about 10 tons (9.7 metric tons).

FACT○SAUR

Paleontologists have unearthed several almost complete fossil skeletons of Shunosaurus. It is one of the best-known sauropods.

Shunosaurus had a club at the end of its long, strong tail. Some Shunosaurus tails even had spikes. An attacker whacked by this heavy weapon was likely to have been badly injured or even killed.

Unlike many sauropods, Shunosaurus had front and hind legs that were about the same length. As a result, its back was level with the ground.

30

Apatosaurus
(ah-PAT-o-SAWR-us)
Apatosaurus lived in western North America. It was a mighty dinosaur, growing up to 80 feet (24 meters) long and weighing a hefty 33 tons (30 metric tons), slightly larger than its close relative Brontosaurus (see page 27).

FUN FACT
The first skeleton of Apatosaurus displayed in a museum had the skull of a Camarasaurus. Many years passed before scientists discovered the mistake.

Camarasaurus
(kam-ah-rah-SAWR-us)
Camarasaurus is one of the best-known sauropods. Many of its fossils have been found in western North America. This dinosaur had hollow spaces in the bones of its neck and head, making them lighter and easier to move about.

> **FUN FACT**
>
> Today, most scientists think the fossils called Seismosaurus are actually just a very large specimen of Diplodocus.

Seismosaurus
(SIZE-moe-SAWR-us)
Seismosaurus means "earthquake lizard." It's a good name for this enormous dinosaur, which grew to about 150 feet (45 meters) long and weighed 85 tons (77 metric tons). It really may have caused the ground to rumble as it walked.

Omeisaurus
(OH-may-SAWR-us)
Old illustrations of Omeisaurus often show a club at the end of the tail. Scientists now think Omeisaurus lacked such a club and that its fossil remains were mixed up with the tail of a Shunosaurus.

Supersaurus (SUE-per-SAWR-us)

is known from only a few fossilized bones. The size of these bones suggests that this supersized dinosaur grew to a length of some 98 feet (30 meters) and a weight of 56 tons (51 metric tons).

UP CLOSE

FACT O SAUR

The fossils of Supersaurus include bones that were once called Ultrasaurus. Only later did scientists realize the bones all belonged to one animal.

Like other large sauropods, Supersaurus probably spent most of each day eating. To save time and gather more food, Supersaurus did not chew its food. Instead, it tore leaves off trees and swallowed them whole.

Supersaurus had a very long neck and a very long tail. It was not the largest or heaviest sauropod, but it was one of the longest.

A single neckbone of Supersaurus stands more than 4 feet (1.2 meters) tall.

33

Cretaceous Sauropods

Sauropods were the largest, most common plant-eaters throughout much of the world for millions of years. Toward the end of the Jurassic Period, many died out. In the Cretaceous Period, which lasted from about 145 million to 66 million years ago, new kinds of plant-eating dinosaurs appeared and began competing with the remaining sauropods.

Sauropods had been common all over the world in the Jurassic Period, but in the Cretaceous Period almost all of them lived in the south, on the supercontinent scientists call Gondwana. This landmass was made up of present-day South America, Africa, Australia, and parts of Asia. The Cretaceous sauropods were also different from the Jurassic ones. Most of them belonged to a new group called the *titanosaurs*. They had sturdier bodies and legs than many of the Jurassic sauropods, but their necks and tails were shorter. Many of the titanosaurs also developed armor. Their skin was covered with round, bony plates. These bony plates offered good protection from large, meat-eating dinosaurs. Titanosaurs were also protected by their great size. Most were simply too large for any meat-eater to take down. However, the young were vulnerable, and many were probably eaten before they were fully grown.

Nearly all Cretaceous sauropods, such as Jobaria from Africa *(left)*, thrived in the Southern Hemisphere. Only a few, such as Pelorosaurus *(opposite)*, lived in the Northern Hemisphere.

35

Aeolosaurus

(EE-oh-lo-SAWR-us)
Scientists think Aeolosaurus may have lived in herds, like many other sauropods. The herds would migrate to different feeding areas depending on the season.

FUN FACT

Paleontologists have found preserved skin impressions of Pelosaurus that show this sauropod was covered with *hexagonal* (six-sided) plates of tough skin.

Pelorosaurus

(pe-LOW-roh-SAWR-us)
Pelorosaurus was one of the first long-necked sauropods to be discovered. Its fossils were first found in Europe, in the United Kingdom, in 1849. It lived about 135 million years ago.

Amargasaurus (uh-MARG-uh-SAWR-us)

lived in what is now South America about 125 million years ago. It was a relative of Diplodocus. Scientists think it probably fed on soft, low-growing ferns.

UP CLOSE

FACT O SAUR

The spikes of Amargasaurus may have served as protection, but some scientists think they may have been for show.

Amargasaurus had two rows of spines running down its neck. Reaching as long as 20 inches (51 centimeters), these spines may have provided a defense against meat-eating dinosaurs.

Amargasaurus had long and slender teeth that grew only at the front of the mouth. It had a rather short neck for a sauropod.

Antarctosaurus
(ant-ARK-toe-SAWR-us)
Antarctosaurus could stretch up and pull leaves off branches that were 20 feet (6.5 meters) above the ground. It had teeth only at the front of its mouth, so it was unable to chew food.

FUN FACT
The first dinosaur eggs ever discovered were the fossilized eggs of Hypselosaurus, in 1869. At first, scientists thought the eggs were laid by a giant prehistoric bird.

Hypselosaurus
(HIP-sel-oh-SAWR-us)
Hypselosaurus eggs were about 12 inches (30 centimeters) across. Scientists think that Hypelosaurus carefully positioned its eggs in the nest, because the eggs have been found in a tight clutch.

Argentinosaurus (ahr-gen-TEEN-oh-SAWR-us),

found in the South American country Argentina, was the largest land animal that ever lived. Although Argentinosaurus lived among gigantic meat-eating dinosaurs, it was at no risk of being hunted and eaten as an adult. This sauropod was simply too large to attack.

UP CLOSE

Argentinosaurus grew to a length of up to 135 feet (41 meters) and a weight of as much as 90 tons (82 metric tons)! Its thighbone alone was more than 8 feet (2.5 meters) long.

Argentinosaurus fossils were found in present-day Argentina, where it lived about 100 million years ago. It fed on the leaves of trees and shrubs. It needed to eat huge amounts of plant matter every day.

FACT O SAUR

Fossils of Argentinosaurus are found in the same region as fossils of Giganotosaurus, one of the largest meat-eating dinosaurs that ever lived.

Argentinosaurus laid eggs on the ground. The young were quite small compared with the adults. Scientists think the adults did not provide care for their offspring.

Magyarosaurus
(MAG-yar-o-SAWR-us)
Magyarosaurus was a "dwarf" sauropod—it grew to "only" about 26 feet (8 meters) in length. Fossils of this dinosaur were found in what is now Romania in eastern Europe. Long ago, this region was a group of islands.

FUN FACT
Magyarosaurus was so small because it lived on islands. Large animals isolated on islands often become smaller over time.

Nemegtosaurus
(NAY-meg-toe-SAWR-us)
Little is known about Nemegtosaurus, fossils of which have been found in Mongolia, an Asian nation north of China. It had a very wide body, but its slender neck could reach into thick *foliage* (leaves) for feeding.

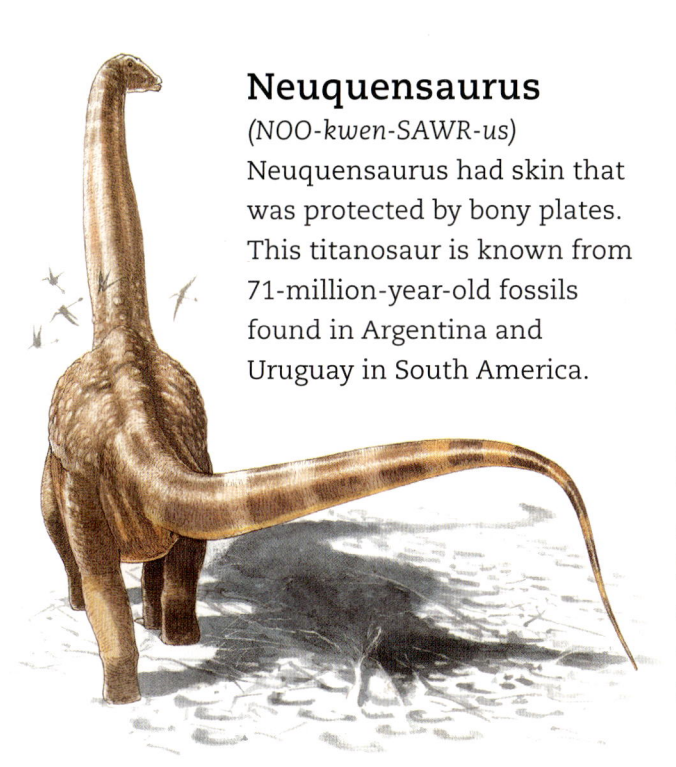

Neuquensaurus
(NOO-kwen-SAWR-us)
Neuquensaurus had skin that was protected by bony plates. This titanosaur is known from 71-million-year-old fossils found in Argentina and Uruguay in South America.

Opisthocoelicaudia
(oh-PIS-tho-SEEL-ih-CAWD-ee-ah)
Opisthocoelicaudia was a stocky, forest-dwelling dinosaur. The name refers to its oddly shaped tailbones, which were hollow. The Opisthocoelicaudia stood on its back legs and rested on its tail, so it could reach high into the trees to feed.

Quaesitosaurus
(kway-ZEET-oh-SAWR-us)
Quaesitosaurus is known only from a single fossil skull found in Mongolia. It was a large sauropod with unusually large ear openings. It may have had keen hearing.

Alamosaurus
(al-uh-moe-SAWR-us)
Alamosaurus could grow up to 70 feet (21 meters) long. Scientists think this dinosaur roamed the land in huge herds.

FUN FACT
During the time that Rapetosaurus lived, at the end of the Cretaceous Period, Madagascar had only recently separated from mainland Africa to become an island.

Rapetosaurus
(rah-PETE-oh-SAWR-us)
Rapetosaurus is one of the last dinosaurs to develop on Earth. Fossils of this dinosaur, found in Madagascar, are only about 70 million years old.

Saltasaurus (SALT-ah-SAWR-us)

was a long-necked sauropod covered in armor. It lived in what is now South America about 80 million years ago. It was about 40 feet (12 meters) long and weighed 3 to 4 tons (2.7 to 3.6 metric tons).

UP CLOSE

FACT○SAUR

In 1997, thousands of fossil dinosaur eggs were found in Argentina. Scientists believe the eggs were laid by a Saltasaurus herd.

Hard, bony plates were embedded in the skin of the dinosaur's back. This would have made Saltasaurus difficult to attack.

No complete skull of a Saltasaurus has been found, but it probably had long, peglike teeth to strip leaves off branches.

Like other titanosaurs, Saltasaurus was powerfully built and had sturdy legs, with a wide, plump body.

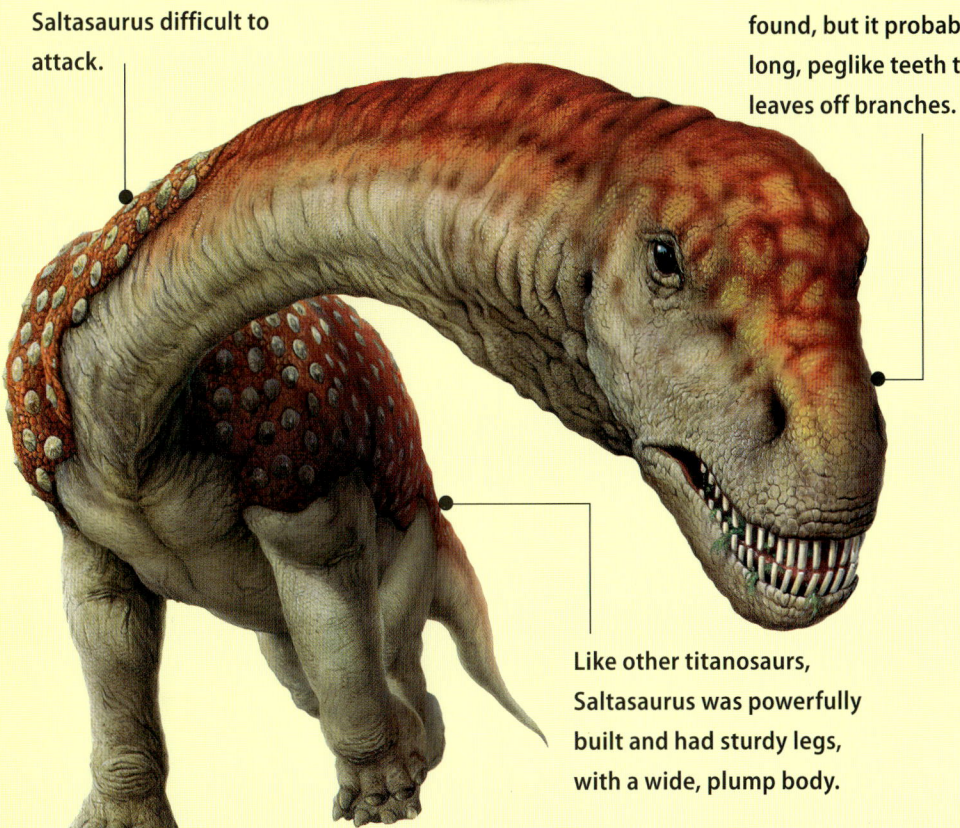

DINO BITE

Why Did Dinosaurs Become Extinct?

For about 160 million years, dinosaurs were the largest and most successful animals on Earth. Then, about 66 million years ago, they disappeared. They died in a mass *extinction* (die off) that affected much of life on Earth. In fact, all animals that weighed more than about 50 pounds (23 kilograms) died out. Many smaller animals also became extinct, along with many plants.

Scientists have developed many theories to explain this extinction. However, since the early 1980's, scientists have uncovered strong evidence that it was caused by the collision of a large asteroid with Earth. (An asteroid is a rocky or metallic object in space smaller than a planet.) The asteroid was at least 6 miles (10 kilometers) across and was traveling at tremendous speed when it struck near what is now Mexico.

The asteroid impact was terrible. It created a crater about 112 miles (180 kilometers) across. It threw billions of tons of dust and debris (other matter) into the atmosphere. Hot debris falling back to the surface may have caused huge fires worldwide. The clouds of smoke and debris would have blocked sunlight from reaching the surface of Earth for many months. The darkened skies likely caused land temperatures to drop below freezing across much of the world. Although the seeds and roots of many plants were able to survive under such harsh conditions, the leaves and other parts of the plants died. Without plants to eat, dinosaurs such as sauropods could not survive. As the plant-eaters died, so did the meat-eating dinosaurs that fed on them.

The sauropods died out with other dinosaurs about 66 million years ago. Scientists have developed a number of theories to explain this mass extinction.

While most scientists now agree that the asteroid was the primary cause of the mass extinction, some scientists believe that other factors may also have played a role. At this time, there were giant volcanic eruptions in what is now India. These eruptions created huge lava beds called the Deccan Traps. These lava beds covered about 200,000 square miles (500,000 square kilometers). The lava beds have cooled to volcanic stone. The beds are more than 1 mile (1.6 kilometers) thick in places. Such enormous eruptions would have released large volumes of gas that caused rapid climate change.

In truth, scientist still cannot explain for why some living things survived the mass extinction while others died out. In fact, most scientists now believe that birds arose from small, meat-eating dinosaurs. Why did certain birds survive the extinction, when other birds and dinosaurs became extinct? Scientists continue to study and debate the causes of the mass extinction that devastated life on Earth about 66 million years ago.

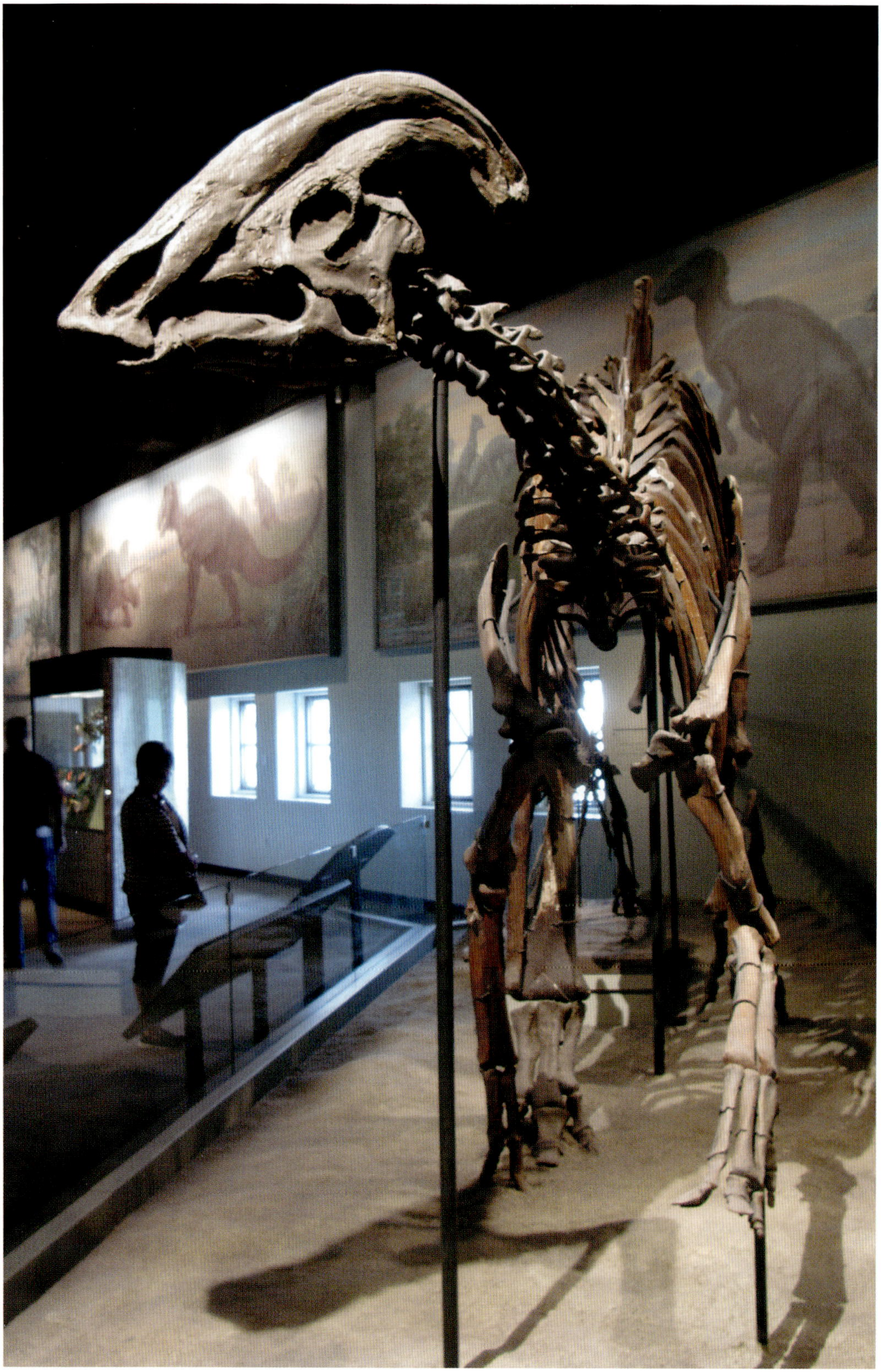

ARMORED DINOSAURS
The Ornithischians

It is a sunny day, about 67 million years ago, in what is now the U.S. state of North Dakota, a state in the central United States that borders Canada. An Ankylosaurus calmly munches low-lying plants along the bank of a shallow river. Suddenly, a fierce Tyrannosaurus bursts through the trees. The Ankylosaurus immediately presses itself to the ground. The Tyrannosaurus lunges to bite, but it can do little damage to the thick, hard armor that protects the back of the Ankylosaurus. Then, the Ankylosaurus pivots and swings its clubbed tail, smashing it into the leg of Tyrannosaurus. The giant meat-eater turns tail and limps away, roaring in pain.

Such was life for the ornithischians (AWR-nuh-THIHS-kee-uhns), which are also known as the *armored dinosaurs*. They

Preserved skin impressions of a hadrosaur *(right)* show that these dinosaurs had thick skin with a pebbly texture. The fossil skeleton of a large hadrosaur called Parasaurolophus *(opposite)* displays an impressive head crest. The head crest was probably used to make loud honking calls.

needed their armor, for these dinosaurs lived among the largest *predators* (meat-eaters) that ever roamed Earth. There were four main types of ornithischians: (1) ankylosaurs (2) stegosaurs, (3) ceratopsians, (4) and hadrosaurs.

Each of these groups thrived for millions of years. Ankylosaurs *(ANG-kuh-luh-sawrz)* had broad heads, tanklike armored bodies, and heavy, clubbed tails. Stegosaurs *(STEHG-uh-sawrz)* grew two rows of spikes or plates along their back and tail. The ceratopsians *(SEHR-uh-TOP-see-uhns)* were horned dinosaurs, resembling rhinoceroses. They had a parrotlike beak and a large bony frill extending across the neck from the back of the skull. The hadrosaurs *(HAD-ruh-sawrz)*, often called *duckbilled dinosaurs*, had a broad, ducklike beak at the front of the mouth. Some sported impressive head crests (see the illustration on page 78). Unlike other ornithischians, hadrosaurs lacked armor. Instead, they lived in herds for protection.

Giant armored dinosaurs lived throughout the Age of Dinosaurs—252 million to 66 million years ago. During this period, Earth went through great changes. In the beginning, a vast supercontinent that scientists call Pangaea *(pan-JEE-uh)* was surrounded by a great ocean. Pangaea broke apart over millions of years, and the continents began to move toward the positions they occupy today. Early in the Age of Dinosaurs, such seed plants as *conifers* (for example, pines and firs), *cycads* (*SY-kadz*—mostly evergreen plants that live in warm climates), and ginkgoes (*GIHNG-kohz*—another non-flowering plant) were common; flying reptiles—pterosaurs *(TEHR-uh-sawrz)*—filled the skies; the oceans teemed with plesiosaurs *(PLEE-see-uh-sawrz)* and other marine reptiles; birds arose from small meat-eating dinosaurs; and the first snakes appeared, along with modern bony fish.

Some ornithischians thrived during these changes, while others struggled to adapt. The stegosaurs had all but disappeared by the Cretaceous Period. Scientists are not sure why they went into decline, but they may have struggled to compete with other plant-eating dinosaurs. The ankylosaurs, ceratopsians, and hadrosaurs are among the most common fossils of dinosaurs from the Cretaceous Period. They flourished right up until the end of the Age of Dinosaurs, about 66 million years ago. At this time, the dinosaurs became extinct. The armored giants that once roamed the land have all died, but we can reconstruct their world through the fossils they left behind.

A life-sized model of the dinosaur Chasmosaurus.

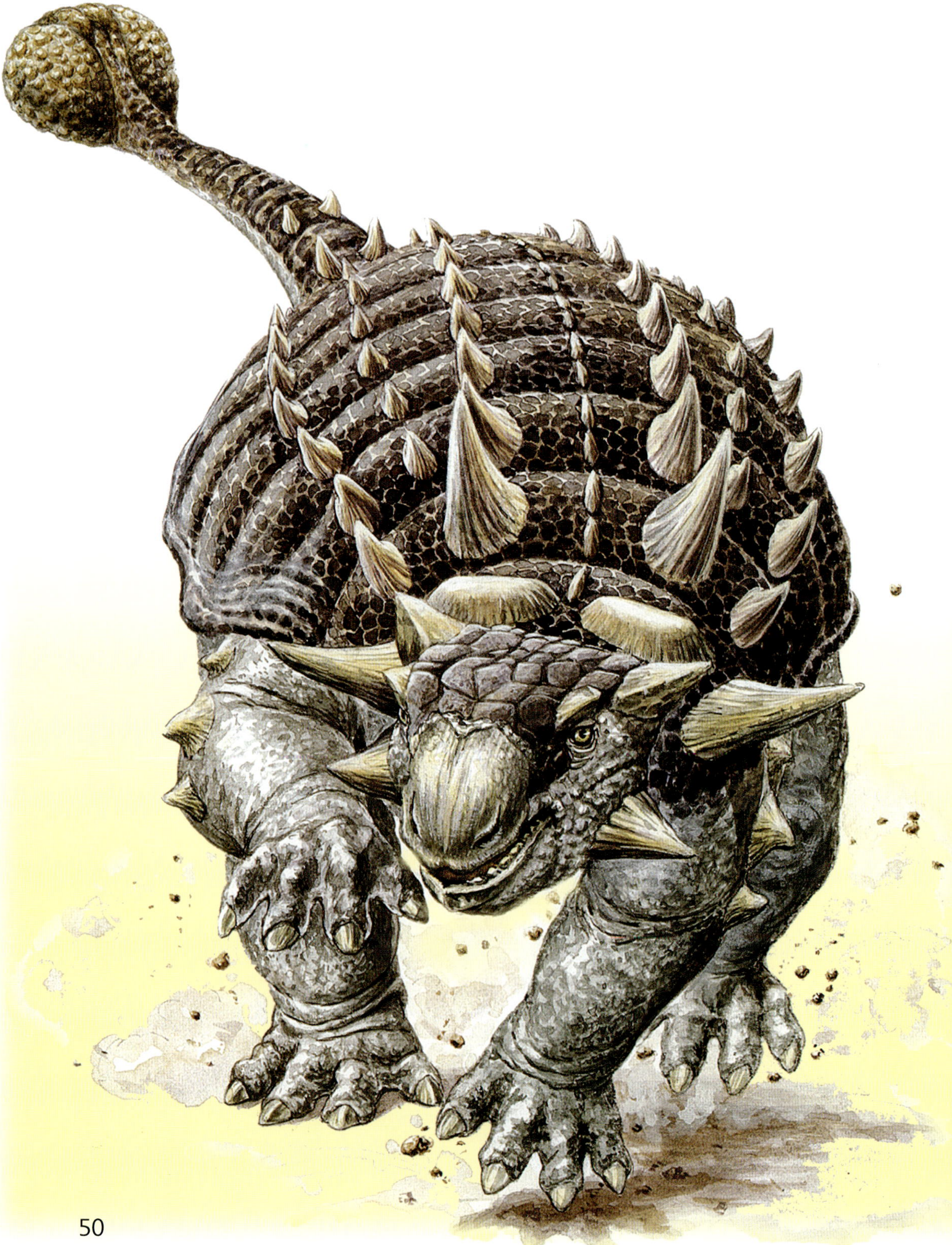

Ankylosaurs

The ankylosaurs were the most heavily armored of all dinosaurs. They needed a lot of protection because they lived in a world full of fierce meat-eating dinosaurs. Ankylosaurs were low, broad animals that walked on four legs. This made it almost impossible for predators to tip them over and attack their soft bellies. Most ankylosaurs had heavy, bony plates embedded in the skin across their back, tail, and head. Many of the plates had ridges or spikes. In some ankylosaurs, large spikes also grew at the shoulders or at the back of the head. Some even had armored eyelids! Many ankylosaurs had a large mass of bone at the end of the tail. This bone could be used as a powerful club to defend against predators.

Although most ankylosaurs were large and walked on all fours, some early kinds were much smaller and lightly armored. These early ankylosaurs could probably move about on either two or four legs.

Ankylosaurs lived in many parts of the world from the early Jurassic Period to the end of the Cretaceous Period. These tanklike animals were some of the most successful plant-eating dinosaurs. They ate the leaves of ferns and low-growing plants, which they sheared off with their pointed, horny beaks. The ankylosaurs died out with other dinosaurs at the end of the Cretaceous Period, about 66 million years ago.

Many ankylosaurs had a bony club at the end of the tail and sharp spikes on their bodies for defense *(opposite)*. Here *(right)*, a fossilized tail club is pictured.

Hylaeosaurus
(hi-LEE-oh-SAWR-us)
Hylaeosaurus was the first ankylosaur fossil found in the United Kingdom, in 1832. It weighed up to about 1 ton (0.9 metric ton) and was heavily armored, with bony plates and spikes.

Dracopelta
(drack-oh-PELL-ta)
Dracopelta could rely on its bony covering and sharp body spikes for protection from attack. This small, early ankylosaur may have rolled into an armored ball when attacked.

Emausaurus
(EE-mau-SAWR-us)
Emausaurus had leaf-shaped teeth that it used to pull large amounts of leaves from branches. Much of its body was covered in bony scales.

Scelidosaurus (SKEL-eye-doh-SAWR-us)

was a small, armored dinosaur that lived about 200 million years ago. Scientists have found its fossils in Asia, Europe, and North America. It was among the earliest ankylosaurs.

UP CLOSE

FACT O SAUR

Sir Richard Owen was a British scientist who named Scelidosaurus in 1860. He also coined the term "dinosaur"—"terrible lizard"—in 1842.

Scelidosaurus shared its environment with a number of large predators, but its armor plates would have made it difficult to attack.

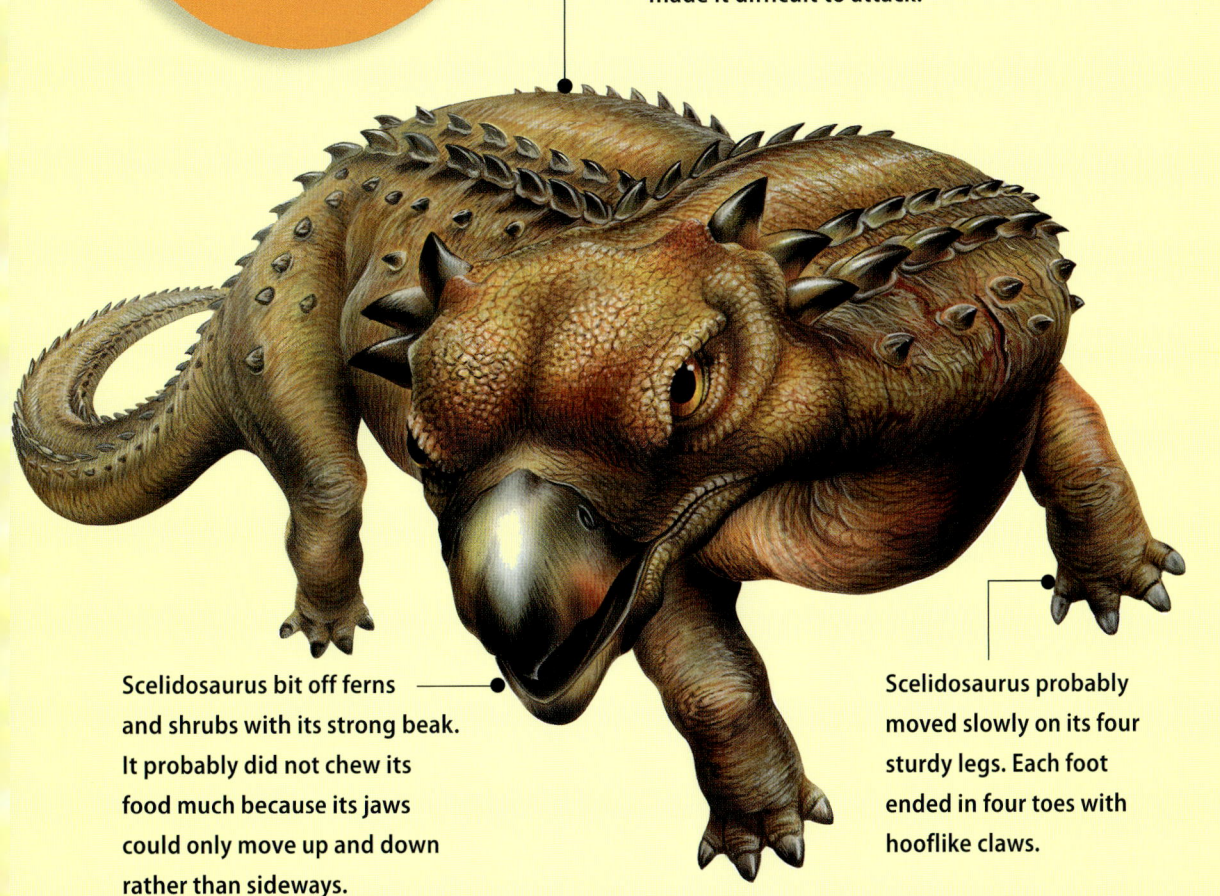

Scelidosaurus bit off ferns and shrubs with its strong beak. It probably did not chew its food much because its jaws could only move up and down rather than sideways.

Scelidosaurus probably moved slowly on its four sturdy legs. Each foot ended in four toes with hooflike claws.

53

Polacanthus
(pole-ah-CAN-thus)
Polacanthus weighed about 1 ton (0.9 metric ton). It had evenly spaced rows of spikes along its sides and on its shoulders.

Nodosaurus
(NODE-oh-SAWR-us)
Nodosaurus means "knobbly lizard." These armored giants were given their name because of their hard shell of knob-covered bony plates. Nodosaurus and its close relatives lacked a bony club at the end of the tail.

Minmi
(MIN-mee)
Fossils of Minmi were first discovered in Queensland, Australia. This small, early ankylosaur is known from several nearly complete skeletons.

Saichania
(siy-KAHN-ee-ah)
Saichania had empty chambers in its skull, which suggests that it had an excellent sense of smell. These spaces also may have allowed it to roar loudly.

Struthiosaurus
(STROO-thee-oh-SAWR-us)
Struthiosaurus is the smallest armored dinosaur known. An adult measured about 6 feet (2 meters) long from head to tail.

Talarurus
(TAL-a-RU-rus)
Large meat-eaters probably thought twice before attacking Talarurus. Biting through Talarurus's bony plates would have been difficult. This dinosaur could also swing the club on its tail like a hammer to smash even the thick bones of a big attacker.

FUN FACT
The tail of Talarurus had *tissues* (cells that make up the body of animals or plants) interwoven like a basket. This provided great power and strength when swinging the tail against an attacker.

Euoplocephalus
(YOU-oh-plo-SEF-ah-lus)
Euoplocephalus had a crushing disc-shaped tail club that weighed more than 30 pounds (13.6 kilograms).

Edmontonia
(ed-mon-TOE-nee-ah)
Edmontonia had two huge spines on each shoulder. One pointed forward to protect the head and neck. The other pointed backward to protect the sides. With no club on the tail, this armored ankylosaur may have faced predators head-on.

Panoplosaurus
(PAN-oh-ploh-SAWR-us)
Like most ankylosaurs, Panoplosaurus had a toothless beak for feeding on low plants. It was a massive animal, weighing up to $3\frac{1}{2}$ tons (3.2 metric tons).

FUN FACT
The skull of Panoplosaurus shows it likely had fleshy cheek pouches. These were used to hold plant matter, which the animal chewed slowly but constantly.

FACT O SAUR

When attacked, Ankylosaurus may have pressed itself to the ground. In this position, the attacker could only bite or claw at the tough armor.

Ankylosaurus
(ANG-kuh-luh-SAWR-us)

was built like a tank! Its head and back were covered with bony plates and long spikes, and it had an intimidating bone club at the end of its tail.

UP CLOSE

Ankylosaurus had a globe-shaped club on the tail that was nearly the same size as its head. It could swing this club with great force.

Ankylosaurus lived in North America from 66 million to 68 million years ago. Its massive armor helped to protect it from such huge meat-eating dinosaurs as Tyrannosaurus.

Ankylosaurus was the largest armored dinosaur. It grew to about 33 feet (10 meters) long and weighed up to 8 tons (7.3 metric tons).

Stegosaurs

The stegosaurs were a striking group of dinosaurs. Some of them looked odd, with a heavy body, a small head, long hind legs, and large plates sticking up from the back. Indeed, the name stegosaur means "roof reptile," because the large plates resemble roof tiles. However, not all stegosaurs had plates on their back. Some had long spikes running along their back and tail.

Some scientists believe that the plates and spikes of stegosaurs were used for defense against predators. Others suggest that the plates helped to control the animals' body temperature. According to this idea, blood passed through the thin plates, where it was cooled by air moving around the stegosaur's back. In this way, the dinosaur could lower its body temperature. The plates could also have helped to warm the blood by absorbing heat from the sun.

Stegosaurs had weak teeth in their long, narrow head. Their short front legs kept the head near the ground, and scientists think stegosaurs fed mainly on soft, low-growing ferns. These dinosaurs reached their peak in the Jurassic Period, but only a few kinds survived into the Cretaceous Period. Scientists are not sure why stegosaurs died out. However, they suspect that stegosaurs may have struggled to compete with other plant-eating dinosaurs.

Stegosaurs kept their long, horselike skull *(opposite)* low to the ground, to feed on low-growing plants. These dinosaurs had a large, heavy body and walked on all fours. The hindlimbs were longer than the forelimbs, which gave them a highly arched back *(above)*.

Huayangosaurus
(hwah-YANG-oh-SAWR-us)
Huayangosaurus was an early stegosaur known from Jurassic fossils found in China. It has many primitive (early, or less evolved) features and may be an ancestor to stegosaurs that appeared later.

Lexovisaurus
(lek-SOH-vee-SAWR-us)
Lexovisaurus was an early, medium-sized stegosaur that lived about 164 million years ago in what are now the European nations of England and France.

Chialingosaurus
(CHEE-ah-LING-ah-SAWR-us)
Chialingosaurus was a medium-sized early stegosaur known from fossils found in China. It probably ate soft, low-growing ferns and plants called *cycads*, which were plentiful in the Jurassic Period.

FACT○SAUR

Although Stegosaurus was huge, it had a tiny brain. Its brain was only about the size of a golf ball.

Stegosaurus

(STEHG uh SAWR uhs)

was the largest of the stegosaurs, growing to 30 feet (9 meters) in length and weighing about 3 tons (2.7 metric tons). It lived in what are now Europe and North America.

UP CLOSE

Two rows of large, triangle-shaped plates lined the back of Stegosaurus. Some plates were more than 3 feet (1 meter) long.

Stegosaurus had a tiny, narrow head. Its toothless beak cropped plants low to the ground. It also had small, leaf-shaped teeth at the back of its mouth.

The end of the tail had four long, pointed spikes. Stegosaurus could swing these spikes at predators that dared to attack it.

FUN FACT

Some fossil bones from the large, meat-eating dinosaur Allosaurus show injuries that match the shape of stegosaur tail spikes.

Kentrosaurus
(KEN-troh-SAWR-us)
Kentrosaurus is known from fossils in Africa. It had plates and spikes along its back and tail, and two more spikes jutting out from its hips. The hip spikes protected the dinosaur's sides from attack.

Dacentrurus
(dah-sen-TROO-rus)
Dacentrurus had two rows of plates along its back and long spikes on its tail. The razor-sharp tail spikes were effective defensive weapons against predators.

Wuerhosaurus (woo-AYR-hoh-SAWR-us)

was among the last of the dinosaurs with plates on the back. It is known from fossils found in China that date to the early Cretaceous Period. Nearly all other stegosaurs had already become extinct earlier, by the end of the Jurassic Period.

UP CLOSE

FACT O SAUR

Wuerhosaurus may have had its armored plates arranged in matching pairs. Other stegosaurs had plates in alternating pairs.

The plates on the back were longer and more rectangular than those that grew on Stegosaurus.

Wuerhosaurus had a small head, wide hips, short forelegs, and a highly arched back.

Ceratopsians

The horned ceratopsians *(SEHR-uh-TOP-see-uhns)* are some of the most famous dinosaurs. Most people recognize Triceratops *(try SEHR uh tops)* as soon as they see it. However, not all ceratopsian dinosaurs were so large and distinctive. Such early ceratopsians as Psittacosaurus *(SIT-ah-co-SAWR-us)* were tiny and walked on long hindlimbs. But even they had the parrotlike beak and wide head seen in later ceratopsians.

Scientists think horned dinosaurs originated in what is now Asia, where the oldest of these fossils have been found. These animals, known as protoceratopsians, then spread to what is now North America, where they thrived. There, they developed into a variety of animals about the size of rhinos or elephants. They had strong bodies, with short and muscular legs. Their large heads had horns on the nose and above the eyes, with a bony frill protecting the neck.

Triceratops is the most famous ceratopsian, and it was among the most successful. Its long horns, bony frill, and large size helped to protect it from such meat-eating dinosaurs as Tyrannosaurus. Triceratops likely roamed in great herds across western North America about 66 million years ago.

A ceratopsian's massive head *(right)* had a bony frill that covered the neck. The frill might have protected its neck from predators. It also might have been used for display. Ceratopsians ate plants with their parrotlike beaks *(below)*.

65

Brachyceratops
(BRACK-ee-SAIR-uh-tops)
Fossils of this ceratopsian are found in North America. Only fossils of the young have been found, so scientists are not sure what the adults looked like.

Psittacosaurus
(SIT-ah-co-SAWR-us)
Psittacosaurus had a parrot-like beak. Scientists think this primitive ceratopsian was an ancestor of the giant horned dinosaurs that followed.

FUN FACT
Several Psittacosauruses probably laid eggs in one nest, like modern ostriches. In this way, they could share the job of guarding the nest.

Bagaceratops
(BAG-uh-SAIR-uh-tops)
Bagaceratops was a small dinosaur that grew to about 3 feet (1 meter) in length. This ceratopsian is known from fossils found in Mongolia.

Protoceratops (PRO-toh-SAIR-uh-tops)

was a primitive ceratopsian that lacked a nose horn. It lived on the dry plains of what is now Asia about 80 million years ago. Protoceratops lived in herds and fed on low-growing shrubs. More than 100 fossil skeletons of this creature have been found in the Gobi Desert in southern Mongolia and northern China.

UP CLOSE

The neck frill was small compared to other ceratopsians and was probably used more to impress a mate than for defense.

FACT-O-SAUR

Scientists have found a fossilized Protoceratops skeleton locked in combat with a meat-eating dinosaur called Velociraptor.

Protoceratops had a horny beak somewhat like that of a bird. It lacked a horn on the nose.

The long tail indicates that the four-legged Protoceratops came from dinosaurs that walked on two legs. Two-legged dinosaurs needed this long tail for balance.

67

Chasmosaurus
(KAS-mo-SAWR-us)
Chasmosaurus had a huge neck shield, but much of it consisted of just muscle and skin stretched between bones. This made the shield relatively light and easy to carry.

FUN FACT
Many ceratopsian fossils are found together. This indicates that they likely moved in large herds for protection from predators.

Einiosaurus
(eye-nee-oh-SAWR-us)
The well-protected Einiosaurus had two straight horns rising from its neck frill and a single, downward-curving horn on its nose.

Centrosaurus
(SEN-tro-SAWR-us)
Centrosaurus was a massive ceratopsian that weighed up to 13 tons (11.8 metric tons). The large nose horn was a powerful weapon. It lived in what is now North America.

Pentaceratops
(PEN-ta-SAIR-uh-tops)
Pentaceratops had an awesome neck frill that could grow up to 10 feet (3 meters) in length. The huge frill was studded with short spikes. Pentaceratops had the largest skull of any land animal that has ever lived.

Pachycephalosaurus
(pack-ee-SEF-ah-low-SAWR-us)
Pachycephalosaurus, a ceratopsian relative, had an incredibly thick, domed skull surrounded by spikes. It may have used its head as a battering ram to win mates.

Styracosaurus
(sty-RACK-oh-SAWR-us)
Styracosaurus had more spikes and horns on its head than any other ceratopsian. Many of these were long, yet thin. They may have been mainly for display instead of defense.

Leptoceratops
(LEP-to-SAIR-uh-tops)
Leptoceratops was another small, primitive ceratopsian that survived into the late Cretaceous Period. It could probably stand and even run on its hind legs, which were longer than the front legs.

FUN FACT
Scientists have found Montanoceratops nests. Each nest contained 12 fossilized eggs laid in a spiral pattern.

Montanoceratops
(mon-TAN-oh-SAIR-uh-tops)
Montanoceratops was a primitive ceratopsian that lived in large herds during the late Cretaceous Period. It had a small, simple head frill and claws on its limbs. Fossilized Montanoceratops bones have been found only in Montana, a western U.S. state on the border with Canada.

Triceratops (tri-SAIR-uh-tops)

had two horns over its eyes and one horn on its nose. Its name means "three-horned face." A huge, bony frill extended from the back of the skull. Triceratops lived about 66 million years ago in what is now western North America.

UP CLOSE

FACT O SAUR
Triceratops bones have been found in vast numbers in Alberta, Canada, where a huge herd was caught in a flood.

The horns over the eyes were sharp, reaching up to 3 feet (1 meter) long. These may have been used in contests for mates, but some horns show damage from such predators as Tyrannosaurus.

Triceratops had strong, stout legs. It may have charged at threats, as does rhinoceros today.

The horn on top of the nose was short and thick. A parrotlike beak was used to clip vegetation.

71

Many hadrosaurs had large, mostly hollow crests on the skull *(opposite)*. A hadrosaur could stand on its hind legs and crop plant leaves with its wide, ducklike beak *(below)*.

Hadrosaurs

The hadrosaurs (HAD-ruh-sawrz) were a highly successful group of plant-eating dinosaurs. They lived during the Cretaceous Period, mainly in what are now Asia and North America. Some, such as the famous Iguanodon (ih-GWAN-uh-don), weighed as much as a small elephant.

Hadrosaurs are also known as duckbilled dinosaurs. These creatures had long heads with wide muzzles (nose, mouth, and jaw areas). Scientists once thought that they lived in swamps and used their muzzles to strain the water for aquatic plants, as many ducks do today. We now know that hadrosaurs lived on dry land and roamed about in large herds.

Unlike many other large plant-eating dinosaurs, hadrosaurs could chew their food. Their jaws were able to move up and down as well as from side to side. They used their wide, toothless beaks for cropping off plant leaves. They had rows of tightly packed teeth at the back of their mouth that could grind up both soft and coarse plants. These teeth were continually replaced as they wore down or were lost.

Some hadrosaurs had a large crest on their head with passages connected to the nose. Scientists think these dinosaurs could blow air through their crest, making a loud honking noise. They may have used these sounds to attract mates or alert the herd to predators.

Abrictosaurus
(uh-BRICK-tuh-SAWR-us)
Abrictosaurus was a plant-eating dinosaur of the early Jurassic Period in what is now southern Africa. It is among the earliest ornithischians to appear in the fossil record.

Camptosaurus
(KAMP-toe-SAWR-us)
Camptosaurus stood on four legs to feed on low-lying plants, but it could also stand on just its hind legs to eat leaves from taller trees. It had leaf-shaped teeth.

Dryosaurus
(DRY-oh-SAWR-us)
Dryosaurus was a slender ornithischian that could run fast on its two hind legs. This may have helped it to escape predators.

FUN FACT
Hadrosaurs had jaws that could move from side to side. This enabled them to chew their leafy food.

Iguanodon (ig-WAHN-oh-don)

lived about 135 million to 125 million years ago, during the early Cretaceous Period. Discovered in 1822 by Mary Ann Mantell in England, it was one of the first dinosaur fossils ever found. Mary Ann's husband, Gideon, named the dinosaur in 1825.

UP CLOSE

FACT O SAUR
The name Iguanodon means "iguana tooth." The dinosaur's teeth resembled those of modern iguanas.

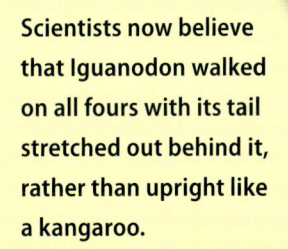

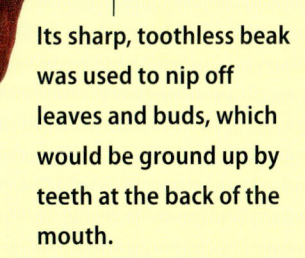

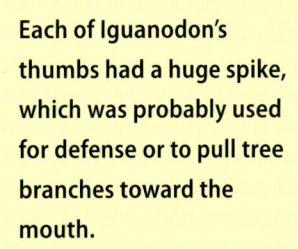

Scientists now believe that Iguanodon walked on all fours with its tail stretched out behind it, rather than upright like a kangaroo.

Its sharp, toothless beak was used to nip off leaves and buds, which would be ground up by teeth at the back of the mouth.

Each of Iguanodon's thumbs had a huge spike, which was probably used for defense or to pull tree branches toward the mouth.

Brachylophosaurus
(BRACK-uh-LOF-o-SAWR-us)
A complete Brachylophosaurus skeleton found in 2000 had been mummified in a sand bank. Its stomach contained fossilized conifers, ferns, and flowers. The skull had a crest of solid bone.

Hadrosaurus
(HAD-roh-SAWR-us)
Hadrosaurus was the first nearly complete fossilized dinosaur skeleton to go on public display (show). Found in the northeastern United States, it was put together and displayed in 1868.

Corythosaurus
(co-RITH-oh-SAWR-us)
Corythosaurus had a large, hollow, bony crest on top of its head. The helmet-shaped crest was probably used to make a loud honking noise.

Maiasaura (MY-yah-SAWR-ah)

lived about 80 million to 75 million years ago in what is now Montana. Its name means "good mother lizard," which refers to the large nesting colonies scientists have found. Maiasaura clearly provided care for its young. It lived in large herds that may have migrated with the changing seasons.

UP CLOSE

The long backbone was stiffened with fibers that helped support its tail, which was used for balance.

Maiasaura could lift itself up on its strong hind legs to reach the tops of trees.

FACT O SAUR

Scientists have found nests with fossilized young Maiasaura. The adults likely brought food back to the infants, as birds do today.

The wide, toothless beak was ideal for cropping off plants, which were chewed by hundreds of small teeth farther back in the jaw.

UP CLOSE

Parasaurolophus (PAIR-uh-SOAR-uh-LOAF-us)

was a large duckbilled dinosaur that lived in what is now North America 75 million to 70 million years ago. Like many hadrosaurs, this animal had a large crest on the skull that could make a loud honking noise.

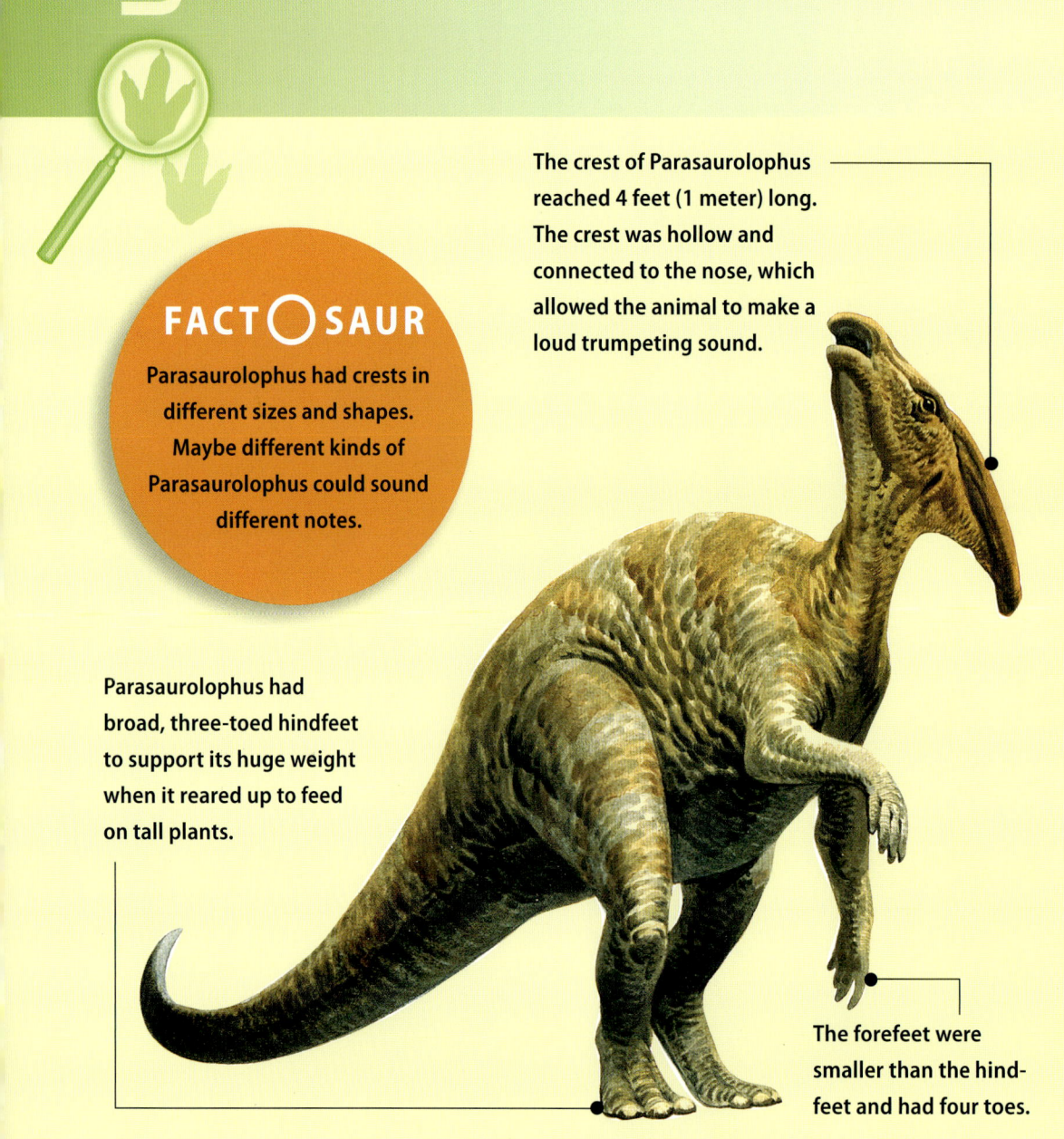

The crest of Parasaurolophus reached 4 feet (1 meter) long. The crest was hollow and connected to the nose, which allowed the animal to make a loud trumpeting sound.

FACT○SAUR

Parasaurolophus had crests in different sizes and shapes. Maybe different kinds of Parasaurolophus could sound different notes.

Parasaurolophus had broad, three-toed hindfeet to support its huge weight when it reared up to feed on tall plants.

The forefeet were smaller than the hindfeet and had four toes.

Lambeosaurus
(LAM-bee-oh-SAWR-us)
Lambeosaurus was the largest of the duckbilled dinosaurs. It had an elaborate, hatchet-shaped head crest. The crest may have been used for display, to attract mates.

Edmontosaurus
(ehd MON toh sawr uhs)
More fossils of Edmontosaurus have been found than those of just about any other dinosaur. These animals were common in the west of North America. The first dinosaur so named was from Alberta, Canada, and was named for Alberta's capital, Edmonton.

Hypacrosaurus
(hi-PACK-roe-SAWR-us)
Hypacrosaurus had up to 40 rows of teeth in its mouth. The teeth wore against each other to stay sharp. A hollow crest may have been used to make loud calls.

DINO BITE

Did Dinosaurs Care for Their Young?

For many years, most scientists believed that dinosaurs provided no care for their young. Early *paleontologists* (scientists who study prehistoric life) assumed that dinosaurs laid their eggs and then left the young to fend for themselves, as most modern reptiles do. However, a series of remarkable discoveries have shown that some dinosaurs were caring parents.

The first evidence for dinosaur parenting came in the 1920's. Paleontologists working in Mongolia discovered many fossils of Protoceratops at a single site, including adults, young, and eggs in nests. This discovery showed that Protoceratops parents nested in groups.

Nearby, the scientists found an ostrichlike dinosaur they called Oviraptor (see pages 117 and 129), which means "egg robber." Paleontologists gave the dinosaur this name because its skeleton was found atop a nest of eggs, which they thought belonged to Protoceratops. Later, scientists examined the eggs more carefully and discovered that they contained tiny Oviraptors. The Oviraptor was not raiding a Protoceratops nest. Rather, it was sitting among its own eggs, tending them much like a modern bird.

In fact, paleontologists have discovered that birds arose from small, meat-eating dinosaurs much like Oviraptor. Some of the nesting behavior we associate with birds may actually have originated among these dinosaurs.

Still, paleontologists do not believe that all dinosaurs cared for their young. For example, the sauropods were the largest dinosaurs, and each of their eggs was about the size of a bowling ball. However, giant sauropods probably did not care for their young, for the simple reason that a hatchling sauropod could easily have been crushed by the lumbering feet of its own parent! Most hatchling sauropods were likely gobbled up by roving predators, with only a few surviving to become adults.

The most famous dinosaur parent is the hadrosaur Maiasaura (see page 77), a name which means "good mother lizard." In the 1980's, scientists discovered the dinosaur's fossils in western Montana among regularly spaced mounds that were lined with vegetation. These mounds were dinosaur nests. Among the nests, scientists found the remains of eggshells, baby hatchlings, and juveniles. Further study showed that the hatchlings had poorly developed leg muscles, and they probably could not walk. But their teeth showed wear that suggests they were eating the same leafy foods as their parents. Thus, paleontologists think Maiasaura parents must have brought food back to the nest until their hatchlings were old enough to fend for themselves. Many other hadrosaurs may have raised their young in similar fashion.

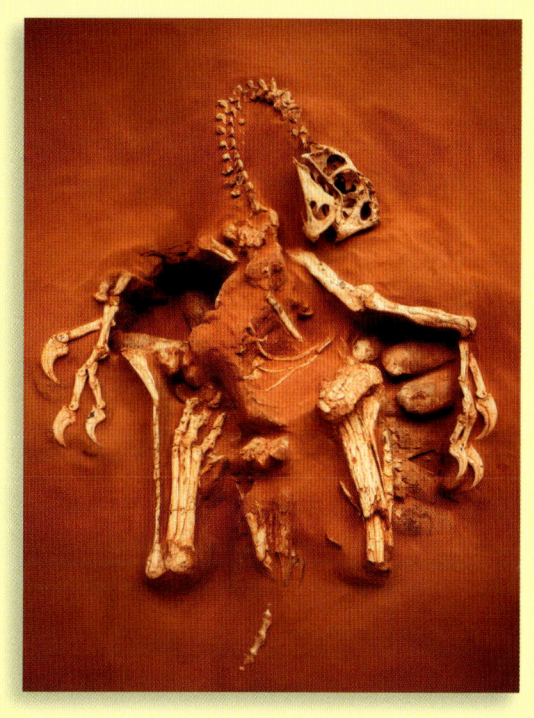

This fossil skeleton of an Oviraptor (above) was discovered atop a nest of eggs. The dinosaur was not raiding a nest. Instead, it was guarding its own eggs.

Paleontologists may never know how many dinosaurs cared for their young, because fossilized nests and eggs are quite rare. Nevertheless, they continue to make remarkable finds that show how dinosaurs lived and reproduced (created young like themselves). Scientists may ultimately find that many dinosaurs were caring parents.

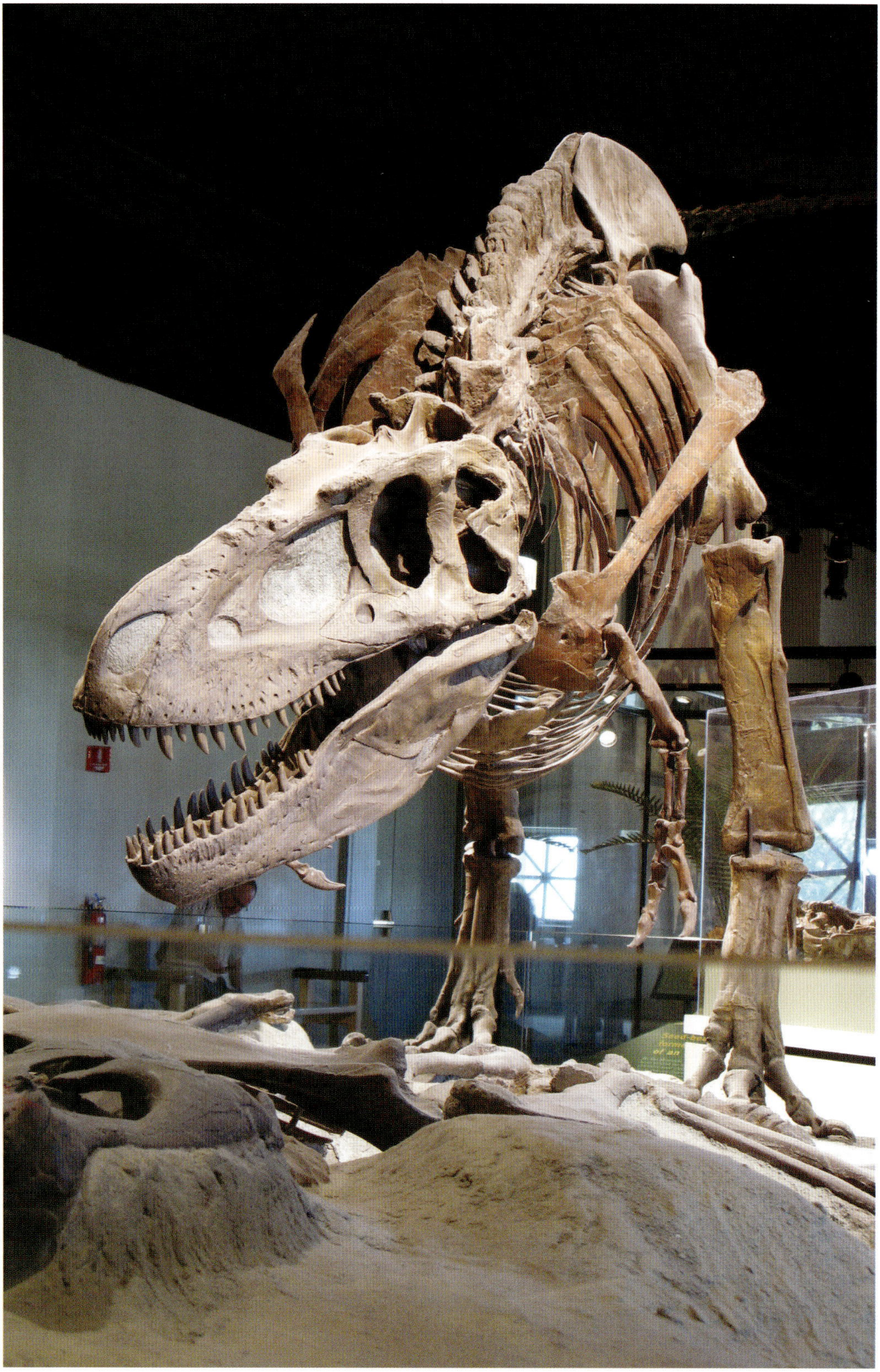

FIERCE DINOSAURS
The Large Theropods

About 150 million years ago, on the plains of what is now western North America, one of the most fearsome *predators* (meat-eaters) of all time hides among the trees, watching a young Stegosaurus eat ferns. Mighty Allosaurus reaches more than 30 feet (9 meters) long and weighs more than 2 tons (1.8 metric tons). The fierce predator readies its dangerous claws, some of which are nearly 10 inches (25 centimeters) long. Suddenly, Allosaurus lunges forward to attack. The young Stegosaurus tries to fight back, thrashing about with its spiked tail. But this Allosaurus is an experienced hunter. It delivers a devastating strike to the neck, toppling its victim. After a few twitches, the Stegosaurus falls still, and the Allosaurus begins to feast.

The long, sharp claw of Baryonyx *(right)* demonstrates the great size and fearsome nature of large theropods. In this skeleton, Daspletosaurus leers over its prey, showing its terrifying teeth *(opposite)*.

Allosaurus was a type of dinosaur called a *theropod* (THAIR-uh-pod). All meat-eating dinosaurs were theropods. Most were powerfully built. Theropods walked upright on their two hind legs, and many kinds could run quickly. Their relatively short arms ended in hands that could grasp objects. Nearly all theropods had a long, muscular tail, which they used for balance. However, theropods varied greatly in size. The smallest theropods were only about the size of a chicken. The largest theropods were far longer and heavier than any predator alive today. Such giant dinosaurs as Allosaurus and Tyrannosaurus had sharp teeth and strong jaws, which helped to make them the most powerful predators of the Age of Dinosaurs, which lasted from about 252 million to 66 million years ago.

Earth went through great changes during the Age of Dinosaurs. In the beginning, a vast supercontinent that scientists call Pangaea *(pan-JEE-uh)* was surrounded by a great ocean (see page 9). Pangaea broke apart over millions of years, and the continents began to shift toward the positions they occupy today. There also were great changes among plants and animals. Early in the Age of Dinosaurs—some 252 million years ago—such seed plants as conifers, cycads, and ginkgoes were common. The first true *mammals* (warm-blooded animals that give birth to live young) appeared, and crocodilians, frogs, insects, and lizards prospered. Flying reptiles called pterosaurs *(TEHR-uh-sawrz)* filled the skies. Plesiosaurs *(PLEE-see-uh-sawrz)* and other marine reptiles ruled the oceans. Later, flowering plants appeared and began to replace other seed plants in some areas, helping insects and mammals to thrive. Birds arose from small meat-eating dinosaurs and soon spread around the world.

Some dinosaurs flourished as conditions on Earth changed, while others struggled to adapt. Allosaurus and many other large theropods went extinct, but many theropods continued to thrive. Near the end of the Cretaceous Period, such large theropods as Tyrannosaurus still ruled the land. However, all these large, fierce dinosaurs died out with the other dinosaurs, about 66 million years ago. Birds were the only descendants of dinosaurs to survive. Fortunately, we can learn about the world of fierce theropods through the fossils they left behind.

A life-sized model of an Allosaurus in Leba Park, Poland.

Triassic Theropods

The earliest-known theropods appeared about 230 million years ago in what is now South America, during the middle of the Triassic Period. In fact, the very first dinosaurs may have been theropods.

Triassic theropods were generally smaller and lighter than later theropods. Early theropods were slender, with flexible bodies and tails. They also generally had weaker claws, teeth, and jaws than many later theropods.

Triassic theropods were active, quick runners. They had to compete with many other kinds of animals for food and other resources. Many of these early theropods probably ate such food as eggs, insects, lizards, and small mammals. Early theropods had five fingers on their hands, though for many of them, the fourth and fifth fingers were probably too short to be of much use. Later theropods had fewer fingers—usually three—on their hands. Fewer fingers apparently worked just as well for grasping and raking prey.

Triassic theropods initially faced strong competition from reptiles and other animals. By the end of the Triassic Period, theropods had become the largest meat-eating animals on land.

A scientist carefully cleans the skull of Eoraptor *(right)*, one of the earliest-known dinosaurs. Eoraptor was a light, swift dinosaur that could chase down small prey *(below)*.

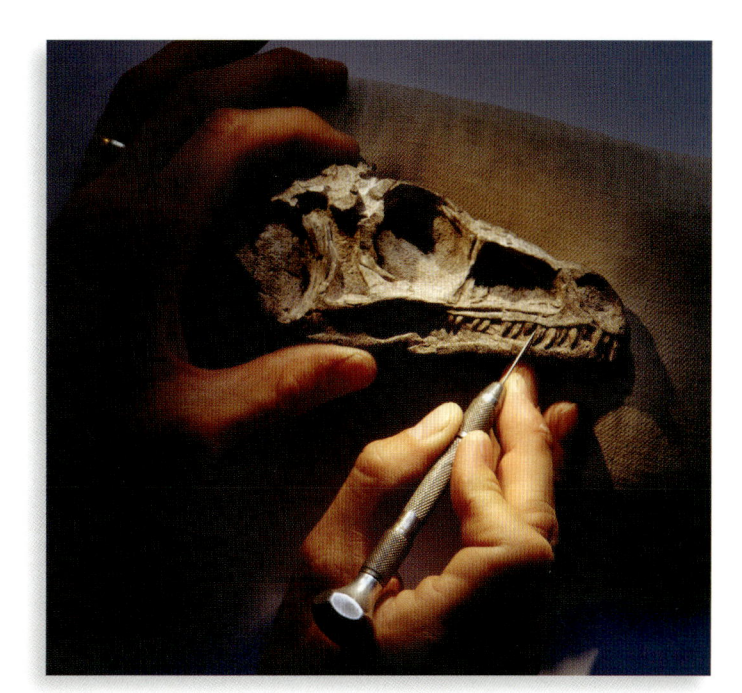

UP CLOSE

Eoraptor (EE-oh-RAP-tor)

is one of the oldest-known dinosaurs. It lived about 230 million years ago, in what is now Argentina. Eoraptor was roughly as big as a medium-sized dog. It had a slender body that reached about 3 feet (0.9 meter) in length. It probably weighed about 20 pounds (9 kilograms). All the later meat-eating dinosaurs arose from creatures much like Eoraptor.

FACTOSAUR

The name Eoraptor means "dawn thief." It first appeared at the dawn of the Age of Dinosaurs. It probably raided nests to steal eggs whenever it could.

Eoraptor dashed around on its long hind legs and used its grasping hands to catch lizards and other small animals. It may also have eaten plants.

Like other predators, Eoraptor had knifelike teeth in its jaws. However, the teeth at the front of its mouth were more leaf-shaped, almost like those of plant-eating dinosaurs.

Eoraptor had five fingers on each hand, though two of them were quite short. Most later theropods had only three fingers on each hand.

Herrerasaurus

(huh-RARE-ah-SAWR-us)
Herrerasaurus was one of the earliest dinosaurs, appearing about 230 million years ago.

FUN FACT

Herrerasaurus lived in deep, thick forests. It may have hidden among the trees until the moment was right to rush out and attack prey.

Staurikosaurus

(STORE-ee-koh-SAWR-us)
Staurikosaurus was a smaller theropod. It was probably a very fast predator that could chase down lizards and other small animals.

Coelophysis
(SEE-low-FIE-sis)
Coelophysis was a graceful, fast-moving predator, with large eyes to help it find prey. It may have lived and hunted in packs.

FUN FACT
Thousands of Coelophysis bones were found at a site in the United States. The dinosaurs may have died together in a flash flood.

FUN FACT
Saltopus was about the size of a house cat. It was only 2 feet (0.6 meter) long and probably weighed only about 2 pounds (1 kilogram).

Saltopus
(SALT-oh-pus)
Saltopus was a small predator that ran on two legs. It had a long head, sharp teeth, and five clawed fingers. Scientists are not certain that Saltopus was a dinosaur—it may have been a closely related reptile instead.

Lilienternus (LIL-ee-in-STER-nus)

was one of the largest predators of its time. It probably grew to about 17 feet (5.2 meters) long. It weighed up to about 300 pounds (130 kilograms).

UP CLOSE

FACT O SAUR

Lilienternus was named after a German doctor, H. R. von Lilienstern. He made many important fossil discoveries from the 1920's to the 1940's.

Lilienternus had a unusual ridge running along the top of its snout. Although Lilienternus was large for its time, it had a slender body compared with other theropods.

Lilienternus had five fingers on its hands. Each finger ended in a sharp claw. These claws were probably used for both hunting and defense.

Lilienternus ran on its hind legs, and it probably could reach high speeds. It likely ate a variety of small animals, including some plant-eating dinosaurs.

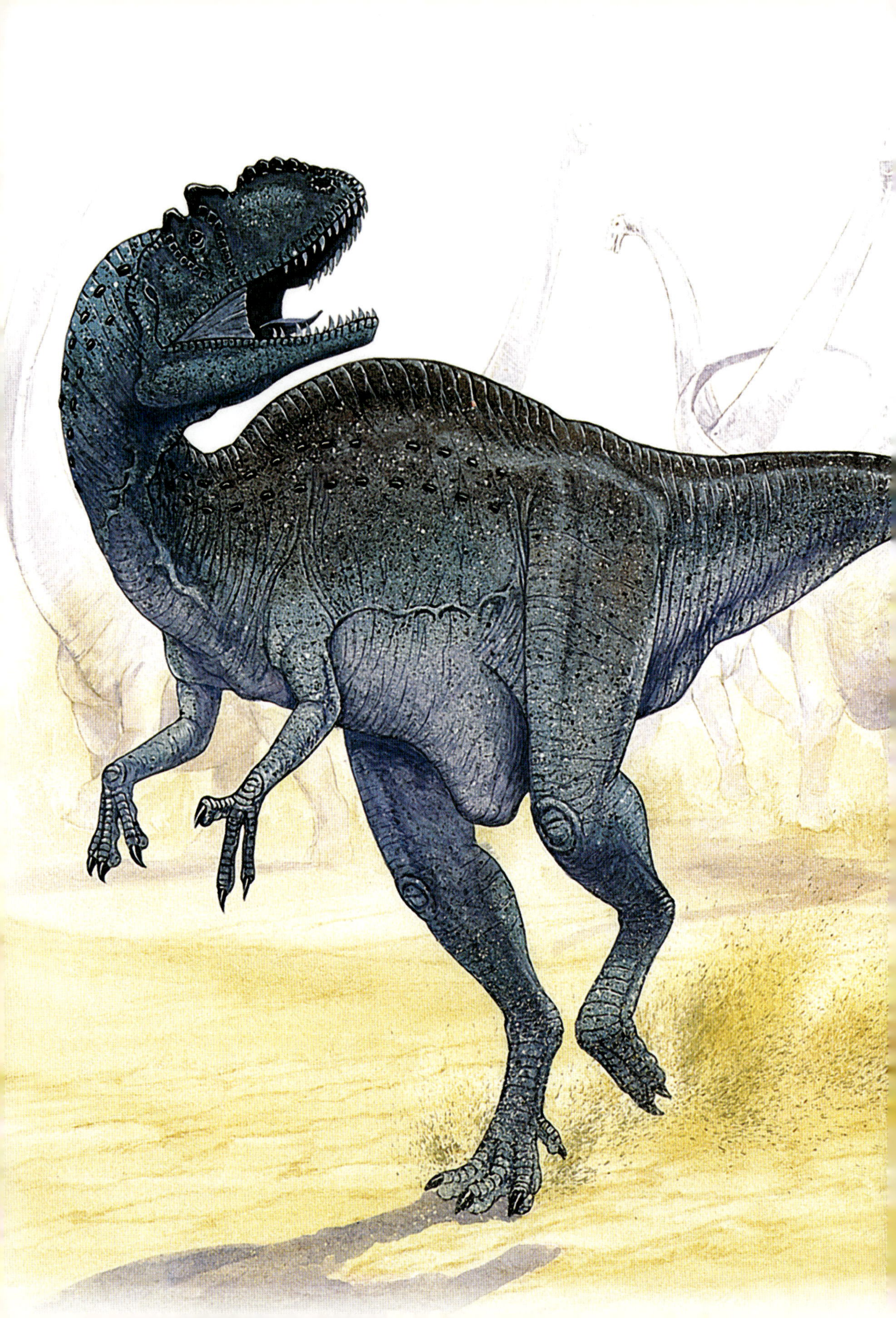

Jurassic theropods such as Yangchuanosaurus *(left)* rank among the largest predators that have ever lived on land. A fossilized skeleton of Allosaurus *(right)* shows the fearsome claws and teeth of this large theropod.

Jurassic Theropods

Theropods became the largest meat-eaters ever to live on land during the Jurassic Period, which lasted from about 201 million to 145 million years ago. Theropods spread throughout the world, becoming the most common predators.

Jurassic theropods were larger and more fearsome than their Triassic ancestors. Their jaws had become stronger, giving them a more powerful bite. Their legs were also more muscular. These features enabled many Jurassic theropods to hunt the enormous plant-eating dinosaurs that became widespread during the Jurassic Period. In addition, some of the Jurassic theropods may have lived and hunted in packs, much like wolves. Many likely hunted during the day, but there is evidence that some theropods hunted at night.

Early in the Jurassic Period, a group of small theropods gave rise to the first birds. In fact, scientists think that many theropods may have had simple feathers. These feathers were generally not used for flight. Instead, scientists believe the feathers provided warmth or were used for display, possibly to attract mates. Theropods also may have been warm-blooded, like modern birds.

Proceratosaurus
(pro-ser-RAT-uh-SAWR-us)
Proceratosaurus was a medium-sized theropod. It had a small crest on its nose, and its teeth curved backward.

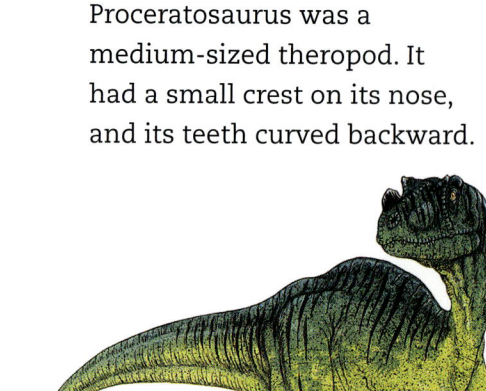

FUN FACT
Cryolophosaurus is one of the few dinosaur fossils discovered in what is today Antarctica, the region surrounding the South Pole—and the only meat-eating dinosaur found there.

Cryolophosaurus
(krie-o-LOF-o-SAWR-us)
Cryolophosaurus had an unusual horizontal crest on its head. The crest ran from ear to ear. It was probably used for display, to attract mates.

Megapnosaurus
(meh-gap-no-SORE-us)
Megapnosaurus was closely related to Coelophysis, and like Coelophysis, it also may have hunted and lived in packs. The size and structure of its eyes suggest that it may have been active mainly at night.

Dilophosaurus (die-loh-foh-SORE-us)

was one of the larger early Jurassic theropods, reaching about 20 feet (6 meters) long. It has often been depicted in movies and video games, but it is often portrayed inaccurately.

UP CLOSE

FACT O SAUR

In the 1993 film *Jurassic Park*, Dilophosaurus had a neck frill and could spit venom. There is no evidence that it had either of these features.

Two long, thin crests grew on top of the head. These may have been used for display, possibly to attract mates.

Dilophosaurus was relatively slender and probably weighed 600 to 1,000 pounds (270 to 450 kilograms).

Dilophosaurus had long, sharp teeth, but its jaw was relatively weak. Its claws were its most useful weapons. Some scientists think Dilophosaurus fed on animal remains, rather than on prey it caught.

UP CLOSE

Eustreptospondylus
(you-STREP-toh-SPON-dy-lus)

was a medium-to-large theropod that lived from about 165 million to 160 million years ago. It probably had a typical theropod body, with small forelimbs, strong legs, and an upright posture.

Eustreptospondylus means "well-curved vertebrae." The name refers to the unusual shape of the dinosaur's backbones.

FACT O SAUR

This dinosaur lived on small islands in the eastern Atlantic Ocean, near what is now the United Kingdom. Scientists think it hunted along the shore.

Eustreptospondylus is known from only one incomplete fossil. Scientists think the dinosaur was likely about 16 to 20 feet (5 to 6 meters) long. However, the bones may have been that of a juvenile, meaning adults would have grown larger.

Megalosaurus

(MEG-ah-lo-SAWR-us)

Megalosaurus was a large theropod. It probably grew to about 30 feet (9 meters) long and weighed 2 tons (1.8 metric tons). It lived in the forests of what is now South America, during the middle of the Jurassic Period.

FUN FACT

Megalosaurus was the first dinosaur to be named, in 1824. Previously, people thought its bones belonged to a giant person!

Piatnitzkysaurus

(pit-NYIT-skee-SAWR-us)

Piatnitzkysaurus was closely related to Megalosaurus, and it lived around the same time. But Piatnitzkysaurus only reached about half the size of Megalosaurus. Also, it lived in forests in what is now western Europe.

Afrovenator
(AF-roh-vee-NAY-tor)
Afrovenator was a large theropod that lived in what is now Africa. Scientists once thought it appeared during the Cretaceous Period. Many scientists now believe it appeared earlier, during the Jurassic Period.

Gasosaurus
(GAS-oh-SAWR-us)
Little is known about Gasosaurus because few of its fossils have been discovered. It was probably a medium-sized theropod. Some scientists think it might actually belong to the same dinosaur group as either Kaijangosaurus or Megalosaurus.

FUN FACT
Employees of an oil company discovered the only known fossil of Gasosaurus. The dinosaur was named for the company's chief product, gasoline.

Ceratosaurus (ser-RAT-uh-SAWR-us)

was a medium-to-large theropod that lived toward the end of the Jurassic Period. It probably grew to between about 16 and 26 feet (5 to 8 meters). It had a series of bony plates on its back that probably served as armor.

UP CLOSE

FACT○SAUR
The name Ceratosaurus means "horned lizard," which refers to the large horn on the dinosaur's nose.

Ceratosaurus had a large bladelike horn on its nose. The horn was probably used for display rather than as a weapon.

Ceratosaurus had a long, flexible tail. This tail would have allowed Ceratosaurus to better move in the water. Scientists think it hunted for prey in streams, rivers, or lakes.

The main weapons of Ceratosaurus were its sharp teeth and its dangerous claws.

UP CLOSE

Allosaurus (al-oh-SAWR-us)

has become one of the most famous of the meat-eating dinosaurs. It was a huge predator, in some cases reaching more than 30 feet (9 meters) long and weighing more than 2 tons (1.8 metric tons).

The massive tail of Allosaurus helped the dinosaur keep its balance. Without its tail, Allosaurus would have fallen flat on its face.

FACT O SAUR

Allosaurus had strong arms with curved claws on its hands. The largest claws on Allosaurus were 10 inches (25 centimeters) in length.

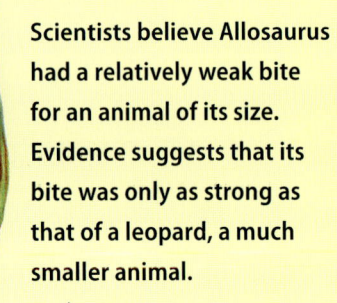

Scientists believe Allosaurus had a relatively weak bite for an animal of its size. Evidence suggests that its bite was only as strong as that of a leopard, a much smaller animal.

Metriacanthosaurus
(MET-ri-ah-CAN-thuh-SAWR-us)
Metriacanthosaurus had a line of thin bones called spines sticking up from its backbone. These spines may have supported a hump or sail-like growth.

Szechuanosaurus
(sesh-WAHN-uh-SAWR-us)
Szechuanosaurus is known only from four teeth, which were discovered in the Szechuan area of southwestern China. Many scientists think the teeth are actually from other kinds of dinosaurs and that Szechuanosaurus was not a unique kind of dinosaur.

Yangchuanosaurus
(YANG-choo-WAN-oh-SAWR-us)
Yangchuanosaurus was a fearsome predator that could grow to more than 30 feet (9 meters) long and weigh more than 2 tons (1.8 metric tons). It had a small crest that ran from the tip of its snout to its eyes.

Cretaceous Theropods

Theropods flourished during the Cretaceous Period, which lasted from about 145 million to 66 million years ago. In fact, we know of more theropods from the late Cretaceous Period than from any other time during the Age of Dinosaurs.

As the continents continued to move apart, the widening oceans created barriers that few animals could cross. Because of this geographic separation, many new kinds of dinosaurs appeared with different ways of life. Some were long-limbed and had toothless beaks to feed on eggs and insects. Some had large claws on their hands and ate fish. Others lived in deserts and probably hunted small mammals and reptiles. The largest theropods were fearsome predators that could attack even the biggest of the giant, plant-eating dinosaurs called *sauropods*.

The large theropods reached their peak with the fearsome tyrannosaurs *(tih-RAN-uh-SAWRS)*, a name which means "tyrant lizard." Tyrannosaurs were very smart, with sharp vision and a keen sense of smell. Their jaws were so strong that they could crush bone. The tyrannosaurs lived in what is now Asia and North America. At the same time, other large meat-eating theropods thrived in what are now South America and Africa. These theropods were the top predators in their lands, just as tyrannosaurs ruled their continents.

The fossilized skull of Tyrannosaurus *(left)* shows its fearsome teeth, which reached the size of bananas. Chilantaisaurus *(below)* was another large, dangerous theropod of the Cretaceous Period.

Baryonyx
(BAYR-ee-ON-iks)
Baryonyx was a large theropod with a skull and snout that resembled those of a crocodile. It probably used its strong, hooked claws to spear fish.

FUN FACT
Fish scales were found in the gut of one Baryonyx fossil. Baryonyx may have spent much of its time hunting in the water.

Becklespinax
(BECK-el-SPY-nax)
Becklespinax (shown at right as a red specimen) is known from only a handful of incomplete fossils. Scientists think it was a large theropod. It may have had a spiny sail along its back.

Suchomimus
(SOOK-o-MIME-us)
Suchomimus had a crocodile-shaped head, large claws, and a sail-shaped growth on its back. It resembled Baryonyx, and some scientists think they may actually represent the same group of dinosaurs.

104

Acrocanthosaurus
(AK-roh-CAN-thuh-SAWR-us)

was an enormous meat-eating dinosaur that could grow to 40 feet (12 meters) long. It weighed from 3 to 7 tons (3 to 6 metric tons).

UP CLOSE

FACT O SAUR

Acrocanthosaurus was the top predator of its time. Scientists have found many footprints in North America that were probably made by this dinosaur.

Acrocanthosaurus had a tall, sail-shaped growth running down the length of its back. This sail may have helped to control body temperature. It also may have been used for display.

The huge head of Acrocanthosaurus was full of daggerlike teeth. The head was more than 4 feet (1.25 meters) long.

Like many other large theropods, Acrocanthosaurus probably had a good sense of smell, which it relied on to find prey.

UP CLOSE

Spinosaurus (SPINE-oh-SAWR-us)

was a gigantic predator that lived in what is now northern Africa. It was probably the largest of the theropods. Some scientists estimate that it reached up to about 60 feet (18 meters) long. It probably weighed about 6 to 9 tons (5 to 8 metric tons).

FACT O SAUR

The first known Spinosaurus fossils were kept in a German museum. They were destroyed by bombs during World War II (1939-1945).

Scientists are not sure why Spinosaurus had a large sail-like growth on its back. It may have helped the dinosaur to control its body temperature. The sail may also have been used for display.

Spinosaurus had a long, narrow snout, like that of a crocodile. Its many sharp teeth were relatively small.

Spinosaurus may have hunted both on land and in the water. The structure of its skull, including its raised nostrils, would have helped it to hunt well in water.

Carcharodontosaurus

(kahr-KAR-o-DONT-o-SAWR-us)
Carcharodontosaurus was one of the largest theropods. It grew to more than 40 feet (12 meters) long, and it likely weighed from 6 to 8 tons (5 to 7 metric tons). It lived in what is now North Africa.

Giganotosaurus

(jie-GAN-oh-toe-SAWR-us)
Giganotosaurus was closely related to Carchardontosaurus and had a similar build. However, it lived in what is now South America, and it was not quite as large.

FUN FACT

Giganotosaurus was not as large as Carcharodontosaurus, but scientists think it had a larger brain.

Chilantaisaurus

(chee-LAWN-ti-SAWR-us)
Chilantaisaurus was a large theropod that lived in modern-day Asia. It had large, hooked claws on its forelimbs. Scientists have only poor-quality fossils of this dinosaur, so many questions remain about how it lived and appeared.

Abelisaurus

(ah-BEL-i-SAWR-us)
Abelisaurus is known from only a single, partial skull found in South America. Scientists think it was a relatively large theropod, probably reaching 25 to 30 feet (7.5 to 9 meters) long.

FUN FACT

The name Alectrosaurus means "unmarried lizard." At the time it was discovered, Alectrosaurus was unlike any other predator found in Asia.

Alectrosaurus

(ah-LECK-troh-SAWR-us)
Alectrosaurus was an early, Asian ancestor of the famous Tyrannosaurus. It was only half as tall, but Alectrosaurus was just as well armed, with large jaws, many teeth, and sharp claws.

Carnotaurus (KAR-no-TAWR-us)

was a large theropod that lived in South America, in what is now Argentina, about 75 million to 70 million years ago. It grew to about 25 feet (7.5 meters) in length and weighed between 1 and 2 tons (0.9 and 1.8 metric tons).

UP CLOSE

The name Carnotaurus means "meat-eating bull." The dinosaur was named for the two stubby, bull-like horns on its head. These might have been used for display or in fights with rivals.

Carnotaurus had long, relatively slender legs with powerful thighs. Scientists think its tail was particularly strong and straight. This combination of features might have allowed it to reach running speeds as fast as 30 miles (48 kilometers) per hour!

FACT O SAUR

Carnotaurus had a massive head, but its jaws were slender and its teeth rather weak. Some scientists think it might have eaten animal remains (already dead bodies).

Carnotaurus had unusually short arms, even for a theropod. Each arm ended in four fingers. The fingers had no claws and could not move.

UP CLOSE

Dryptosaurus (DRIP-toe-SAWR-us)

was a large theropod that lived toward the end of the Cretaceous Period. It probably grew to about 20 to 25 feet (6 to 7.5 meters) in length and weighed from about 1 and 1.5 tons (0.9 to 1.4 metric tons).

FACT O SAUR

Dryptosaurus was the first theropod discovered in North America. Only partial remains of a single skeleton have been found.

The large skull of Dryptosaurus was filled with hollow spaces to reduce its weight.

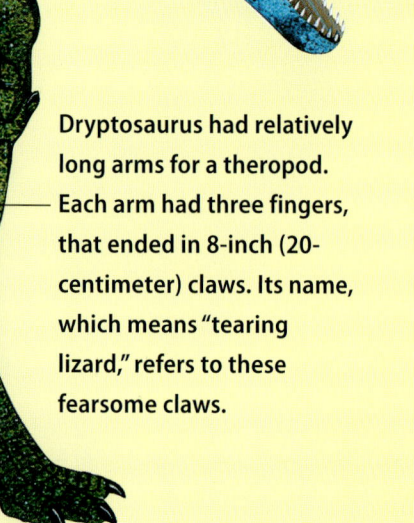

Dryptosaurus had relatively long arms for a theropod. Each arm had three fingers, that ended in 8-inch (20-centimeter) claws. Its name, which means "tearing lizard," refers to these fearsome claws.

110

FUN FACT
Some skeletons of Albertosaurus have been found in large groups, leading scientists to think it hunted in packs.

Albertosaurus
(al-BUR-toe-SAWR-us)
Albertosaurus was a large theropod that lived in modern-day Canada. It was related to Tyrannosaurus. However, Albertosaurus was not as large or as heavy as Tyrannosaurus.

Aublysodon
(aw-BLIS-oh-don)
Scientists have found only the fossilized teeth of Aublysodon. They once thought the teeth belonged to a unique theropod closely related to Tyrannosaurus. However, many scientists now suspect the teeth may belong to another theropod.

Tarbosaurus

(TAR-bow-SAWR-us)

Tarbosaurus was a massive theropod and an Asian cousin of Tyrannosaurus. However, some scientists now argue that Tarbosaurus fossils really belong to Tyrannosaurus.

FUN FACT

The name Tarbosaurus means "alarming lizard." The largest known Tarbosaurus is about the size of the largest-known Tyrannosaurus.

Nanotyrannus

(NAN-oh-tie-RAN-us)

Fossils of Nanotyrannus may simply be those of a young Tyrannosaurus. Nanotyrannus had a large jaw full of serrated teeth and short arms with sharp claws.

Alioramus

(AL-ee-uh-RAY-mus)

Alioramus was another close relative of Tyrannosaurus. However, it was much smaller than other tyrannosaurs, and it had a much weaker bite.

Tyrannosaurus (tie-RAN-oh-SAWR-us)

was one of the most fearsome of all dinosaur predators. It grew to about 40 feet (12 meters) in length and about 12 feet (3.7 meters) at the hips. It weighed about 7 tons (6.3 metric tons). Tyrannosaurus lived in what is now North America.

UP CLOSE

FACT O SAUR

The name Tyrannosaurus means "tyrant lizard." It had one of the most powerful bites of any known land animal. Its jaws could crush bone.

Tyrannosaurus had keen vision, a good sense of smell, and a larger brain than other theropods of similar size. The head was nearly 5 feet (1.5 meters) long, and the teeth were as large as bananas.

Tyrannosaurus held its long tail out to counterbalance its heavy body.

Tyrannosaurus was likely an active hunter that could run a short distance. It may have quietly watched and waited, then lunged at its prey with its powerful jaws and the sharp claws on its two-fingered hands.

DINO BITE What Is a Fossil?

The Age of Dinosaurs ended about 66 million years ago, long before there were human beings on Earth. Yet *paleontologists* (scientists who study prehistoric life) are able to describe how dinosaurs looked and moved. They can tell us about prehistoric forests and strange plants. In museums, we can see the skeletons of dinosaurs that died many millions of years ago. Why haven't their bones turned to dust?

The bones have survived as fossils. Fossils are the remains or the marks of living things that died long ago. The vast majority of plants and animals die and decay without leaving any trace. Such things as bacteria (one-celled living things) break down soft parts such as leaves or flesh, and so these tissues rarely form fossils. Even most hard parts, such as bones, teeth, shells, or wood, are eventually worn away. But when plant or animal remains are quickly buried, they may be preserved from decay. These remains may become fossilized.

Most dinosaur fossils form as part of *sedimentary* (layered) rock. This process begins when dinosaur remains are buried in sediments—that is, the mud or sand that settles out of water. After the remains are buried, water may seep down through the sediments and deposit minerals—iron or calcium, for example—in the bones. Over thousands of years, more and more sediment layers are deposited on the layer containing the fossil. The weight of the upper layers presses down on the fossil-bearing sediment and eventually turns it into rock. Later, wind or water may wear away layers of sedimentary rock, revealing the fossilized dinosaur bones for paleontologists to find.

During the late 1800's and early 1900's, many dinosaur fossils were discovered in Africa, Asia, Europe, and western North America. Today, many new dinosaur discoveries are being made in Argentina, Canada, China, Mongolia, and parts of Africa. These fossil discoveries have greatly increased the number of known dinosaurs. Scientists discover and describe the fossils of several new kinds of dinosaur every year.

Dinosaur fossils usually consist only of bones or other hard parts, such as teeth or armored plates (known as scutes). Rarely, dinosaurs are fossilized

Paleontologist Luis Chiappe works to recover the fossilized skull of a Protoceratops dinosaur in Mongolia.

with softer parts preserved. In 1999, paleontologists working in North Dakota discovered the remains of a hadrosaur named Edmontosaurus that was mummified before fossilization began. Millions of years ago, the dinosaur died on the banks of a sandy riverbed and its body was quickly buried. Waterlogged sediment surrounded the body before it could decay. The fossilized remains were so well preserved that scientists have been able to examine its skin, muscles, and even its internal organs. Other mummified fossils have preserved the remains of the stomach, giving us a look at the dinosaurs' final meals.

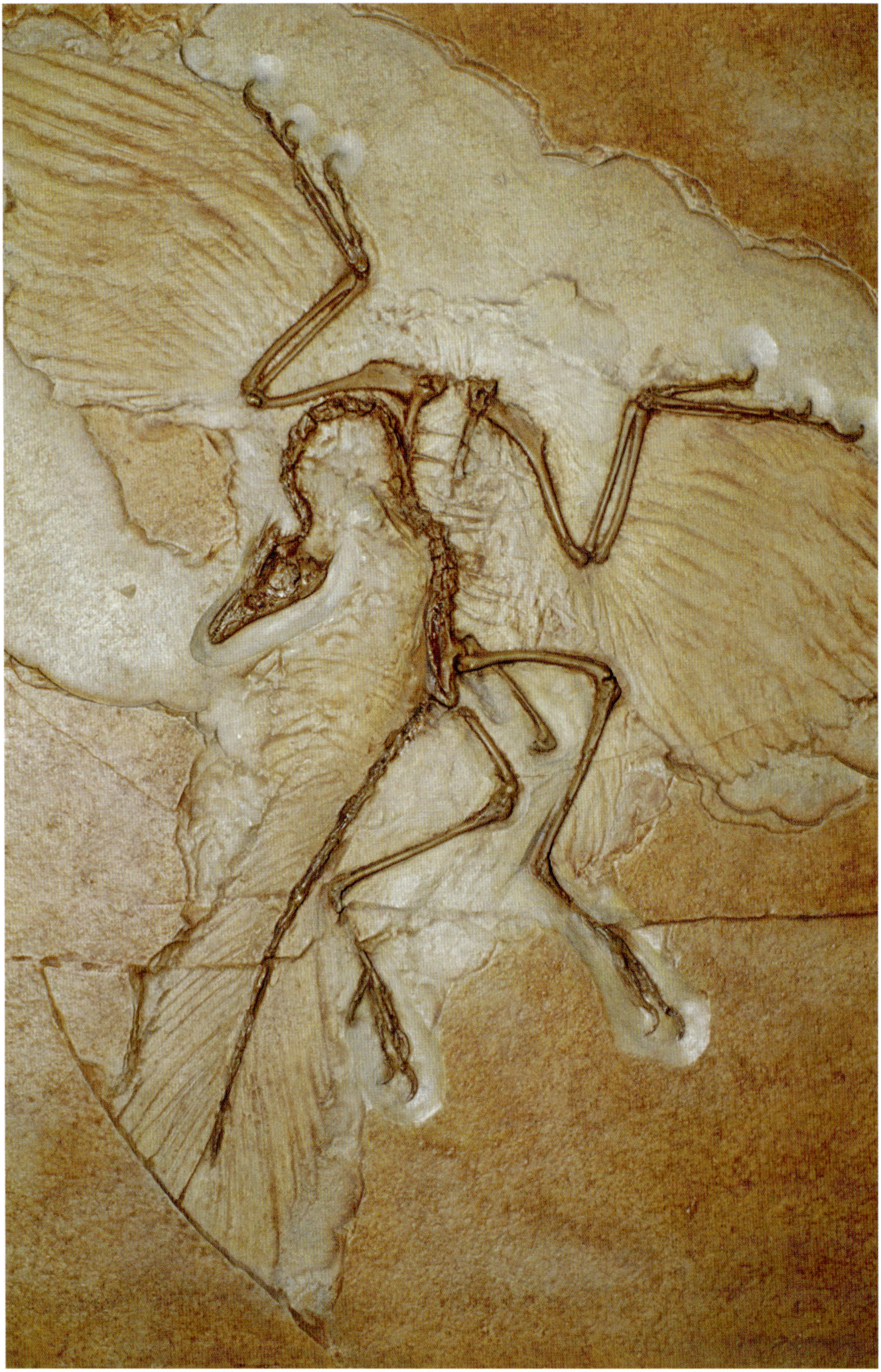

BIRDLIKE DINOSAURS

Small Theropods and Prehistoric Birds

An animal with black feathers watches from the trees, its eyes glittering in the gloom. It is hidden among the leaves of a great forest in what is now eastern Asia, about 120 million years ago. At first glance, the animal appears to be a bird. But as it climbs among the trees, it grips the bark with claws on both its hands and feet. Its jaws are lined with sharp teeth. It seems to have four wings, all with long feathers. When it stretches out its limbs to glide between the trees, it is plain that this animal is like no bird alive today. In fact, it is not a bird at all. It is Microraptor *(MY-kroh-RAP-tuhr)*, a magnificent feathered dinosaur. The discovery of Microraptor and other feathered dinosaurs has transformed our understanding of both dinosaurs and birds.

An egg *(right)* **laid by the dinosaur Oviraptor was recovered from a nest, which the dinosaur guarded, much like a modern bird. A fossil of Archaeopteryx** *(opposite)* **preserves traces of feathers around the animal's body.**

For many years, scientists thought that only birds had feathers—until a feathered dinosaur fossil was discovered in 1996. Other fossil discoveries soon revealed that a variety of small theropod *(THAIR-uh-pod)* dinosaurs had feathers. Most scientists now believe that feathers first appeared among these dinosaurs. In fact, birds descended from one group of feathered dinosaurs. In this sense, birds are feathered dinosaurs themselves.

Theropods were a diverse group of dinosaurs that typically walked upright on their two hind legs. Their relatively short arms ended in hands that could grasp objects. Most had a long, muscular tail to provide balance. However, theropods varied greatly in size. The largest theropods were far longer and heavier than any *predator* (meat-eater) alive today, reaching more than 40 feet (12 meters) long. But other theropods were smaller. Many of the theropods included in this book resembled an ostrich, in both size and body shape. The smallest theropods were only about the size of a crow.

Birdlike dinosaurs appeared some time in the Jurassic Period, near the middle of the Age of Dinosaurs, which lasted from about 252 million to 66 million years go. Earth went through great changes during this time. In the beginning, a vast supercontinent that scientists call Pangaea *(pan-JEE-uh)* was surrounded by a great ocean. Pangaea broke apart over millions of years, and the continents moved toward the positions they occupy today. There also were great changes among plants and animals. Such seed plants as conifers, cycads, and ginkgoes were common early in the Age of Dinosaurs. The first true mammals appeared, and crocodilians, frogs, insects, and lizards grew numerous. Flying reptiles called pterosaurs *(TEHR-uh-sawrz)* filled the skies. Plesiosaurs *(PLEE-see-uh-sawrz)* and other marine reptiles prowled the oceans. Later, flowering plants appeared and began to replace other seed plants in some areas, helping insects and mammals to thrive.

Birdlike dinosaurs thrived up until the end of the Cretaceous Period, about 66 million years ago. At that time, many animals and plants became extinct, including all the dinosaurs except for certain birds. The surviving birds soon developed into many different types and spread around the world. Today, birds are the last living trace of the mighty dinosaurs that once ruled Earth.

A life-sized model of Diatryma, an extinct species of a large, flightless bird.

Sinosauropteryx was a birdlike dinosaur covered in simple, downy feathers. Shadows along the back and tail of a Sinosauropteryx fossil are traces of feathers (right).

Small Theropods

Early birdlike dinosaurs were predators that grew to about the size of a turkey. These small theropods gave rise to a variety of other birdlike dinosaurs of different sizes and with different ways of life.

Many birdlike dinosaurs resembled fierce ostriches. They were light, graceful animals that could run quickly to escape predators. Other birdlike dinosaurs, like Velociraptor, were fearsome predators. Velociraptor had long, intimidating claws on its hind feet that it could use to slash at prey.

These small theropods were like birds in several ways. Their skeletons were similar to those of birds. Most of them probably dug nests in the ground and guarded their eggs. Many birdlike dinosaurs had relatively large brains and were likely intelligent. Like birds, they may have been warm-blooded, which would have made them active and quick.

Many birdlike dinosaurs also may have had feathers. Feathers and soft parts are usually not preserved in fossils, but in rare cases, scientists have discovered traces of feathers around dinosaur skeletons. Many of these feathers are simple, like a chick's downy fuzz. Others are more complicated, resembling modern flight feathers. Some feathers are so well preserved that scientists can even reconstruct their color. Usually, artists have to guess what color dinosaurs were.

In most cases, scientists cannot say for certain whether a particular kind of dinosaur had feathers. But they continue to find more and more small dinosaurs with feathers. It is likely that many of the small theropods pictured in this book actually had feathers.

Compsognathus
(KOMP-sog-NAY-thus)
Compsognathus grew to about the size of a turkey. It had a light body with birdlike feet and short arms. Compsognathus was almost certainly covered in feathers.

Ornitholestes
(or-NITH-oh-LES-teez)
Ornitholestes was a light, slender theropod, which grew somewhat larger than Compsognathus. It had relatively long arms that it could use to grab swift prey.

FUN FACT
Coelurus was among the first birdlike dinosaurs discovered by scientists. Birdlike dinosaurs are also called coelurosaurs in its honor.

Coelurus
(see-LURE-us)
Coelurus was a swift theropod that lived about 150 million years ago. Scientists first discovered fossils of Coelurus in Wyoming in the west of the United States, in the 1870's.

Sinosauropteryx
(SYN-oh-sawr-AHP-tuh-rihks)

was the first dinosaur known to have feathers. These simple, downy feathers held in warmth and could also have been important for mating or other displays. Sinosauropteryx was only about the size of a chicken, growing up to 3 feet (0.9 meter) long.

UP CLOSE

Alternating bands of reddish and white stripes covered the tail.

FACT O SAUR

Scientists have determined Sinosauropteryx's coloration by studying fossils of its feathers with a powerful microscope.

Sinosauropteryx had a very long, bony tail that provided balance when the dinosaur was running.

Pelicanimimus
(PEL-uh-kan-uh-MIME-us)
Pelicanimimus had a deep pouch beneath its lower jaw, like a modern-day pelican. It may have waded into lakes to catch fish. Its jaws held more than 200 tiny teeth, the most of any known theropod.

Utahraptor
(YOO-tah-RAP-tor)
Utahraptor was an unusually large birdlike dinosaur, growing up to 23 feet (7 meters) long. It could slash open prey with the long, sharp claws on its hind feet.

Harpymimus
(HAR-pee-MIME-us)
Harpymimus was an early ostrichlike dinosaur. It had a small skull and long neck. Unlike later ostrichlike dinosaurs, its bill held some teeth.

FUN FACT

Garudimimus is named after Garuda, a large birdlike servant of Vishnu in the Hindu religion.

Garudimimus

(ga-ROOD-uh-MIME-us)
Garudimimus had a toothless bill and likely ate both plants and animals. It had relatively heavy feet and weak legs, so it was not as swift as many later birdlike dinosaurs.

Alvarezsaurus

(al-vuh-rez-SAWR-us)
Alvarezsaurus had birdlike legs and a very long tail. It could run quickly to escape predators. It likely fed on insects.

FUN FACT

Deinonychus and its relatives walked with their long claws held above the ground to keep them sharp.

Deinonychus
(die-NON-ih-kus)
Deinonychus could slash open prey with its claws. A single long claw grew on each hind foot. This relative of Velociraptor may have been covered in feathers.

Erlikosaurus
(ER-lik-oh-SAWR-us)
Erlikosaurus was a plant-eating theropod with long, thin claws. It was a close relative of Nanshiungosaurus.

Nanshiungosaurus
(NAN-shee-ung-ah-SAWR-us)
Nanshiungosaurus belongs to an unusual group of theropods that fed mainly on plants. These dinosaurs had long claws that were likely used for defense and to tear plants.

Velociraptor (va-LOSS-ah-RAP-tor)

was armed with knifelike teeth and sharp claws as well as talons about 6 inches (15 centimeters) long on its feet. It lived about 75 million years ago in what is now Asia.

UP CLOSE

FACT O SAUR

The Velociraptors that were featured in the film *Jurassic Park* were far too large. Actual Velociraptors were only about as tall as a turkey.

Velociraptor grew to about 6 feet (1.8 meters) in length, including the long tail. However, it was only about 3 feet (0.9 meter) tall and weighed only about 35 pounds (15.9 kilograms) when mature.

Fossil evidence suggests that Velociraptor had feathers, though it lived entirely on the ground.

Velociraptor used the long talons on its feet to slash at prey. Some scientists believe Velociraptors may have hunted in packs.

Therizinosaurus
(THER-uh-ZEEN-oh-SAWR-us)
Therizinosaurus had arms more than 10 feet (3 meters) long. Its claws, which reached more than 3 feet (0.9 meter) in length, were far longer than those of any animal alive today. Despite these fearsome claws, this relative of Nanshiungosaurus ate mainly plants.

FUN FACT
Therizinosaurs are sometimes called "sloth dinosaurs," because, like sloths, they ate mainly plants but had long claws.

Conchoraptor
(KONK-oh-RAP-tor)
The roof of this dinosaur's mouth was covered with bony bumps. It may have used the bumps to break open shellfish and tough dinosaur eggs.

Oviraptor (OH-vi-RAP-tor)

was a swift, birdlike dinosaur that lived in what is now Asia. It grew to about 7 feet (2.1 meters) long but weighed only 90 pounds (40 kilograms). Its name means "egg robber," because scientists mistakenly thought it lived on eggs it stole from other dinosaurs.

UP CLOSE

FACT-O-SAUR
Scientists thought Oviraptor stole eggs because they found it in a nest, but they later learned Oviraptor, like modern birds, was actually guarding its own eggs.

Oviraptor had a bony crest on its head. This crest was too weak to serve as armor. Scientists believe it was likely used for display, possibly to attract mates.

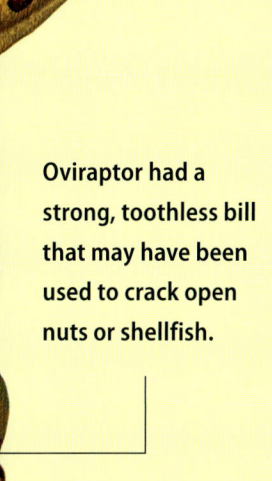

Oviraptor had a strong, toothless bill that may have been used to crack open nuts or shellfish.

129

UP CLOSE

Gallimimus *(gal-uh-MIME-us)*

resembled an oversized ostrich, growing to about 20 feet (6 meters) long and weighing up to 440 pounds (200 kilograms). Gallimimus lived 70 million years ago in what is now Asia.

FACT O SAUR

The name Gallimimus means "rooster mimic," which refers to the dinosaur's birdlike skeleton. But it was much larger than a rooster.

Gallimimus had no teeth in its bill. Some scientists believe it filtered lake and pond water for tiny animals, as many ducks do today. Others think it probably fed on plant matter.

Like an ostrich, Gallimimus had powerful legs that enabled it to run quickly and escape predators.

Chirostenotes
(KIE-roh-STEN-oh-teez)
Chirostenotes was a swift relative of Oviraptor that lived in what is now North America. It probably chased down small mammals and reptiles.

FUN FACT
Borogovia is named after creatures in Lewis Carroll's "The Jabberwocky." He described it as "an extinct kind of Parrot. They had no wings, beaks turned up, made their nests under sun-dials and lived on veal."

Borogovia
(bor-oh-GOH-vee-a)
Borogovia was a small predator that likely ambushed prey, slashing with the claws on its three-fingered hands.

Adasaurus
(ADD-ah-SAWR-us)
Like its close relative Velociraptor, Adasaurus used the claws on its hind feet to attack prey. Adasaurus was about the size of a large dog.

FUN FACT

Scientists found the long arms of Deinocheirus first. It took many years before the rest of its body was discovered.

Deinocheirus
(DINE-oh-KIE-rus)
Deinocheirus was a large, plant-eating theropod with arms that grew 8 feet (2.4 meters) long. The arms ended in strongly curved claws.

Anserimimus
(AN-ser-i-MIME-us)
Anserimimus was an ostrich-like dinosaur with unusually long forelimbs. It grew to only about 3 feet (0.9 meter) long and probably ate dinosaur eggs or small animals.

Archaeornithomimus
(AHR-kee-or-NITH-oh-MIME-us)
Fossilized footprints in China suggest that this dinosaur could run at speeds of up to 43 miles (69 kilometers) per hour, about as fast as a race horse.

Gigantoraptor (jy-GAN-toh-RAP-tuhr)

was by far the largest relative of Oviraptor, growing up to 16 feet (5 meters) tall and weighing as much as 3,000 pounds (1,360 kilograms), about the height and weight of a grown male giraffe. Its skeleton had many birdlike features. Gigantoraptor lived about 70 million years ago in Asia, in what is now Mongolia.

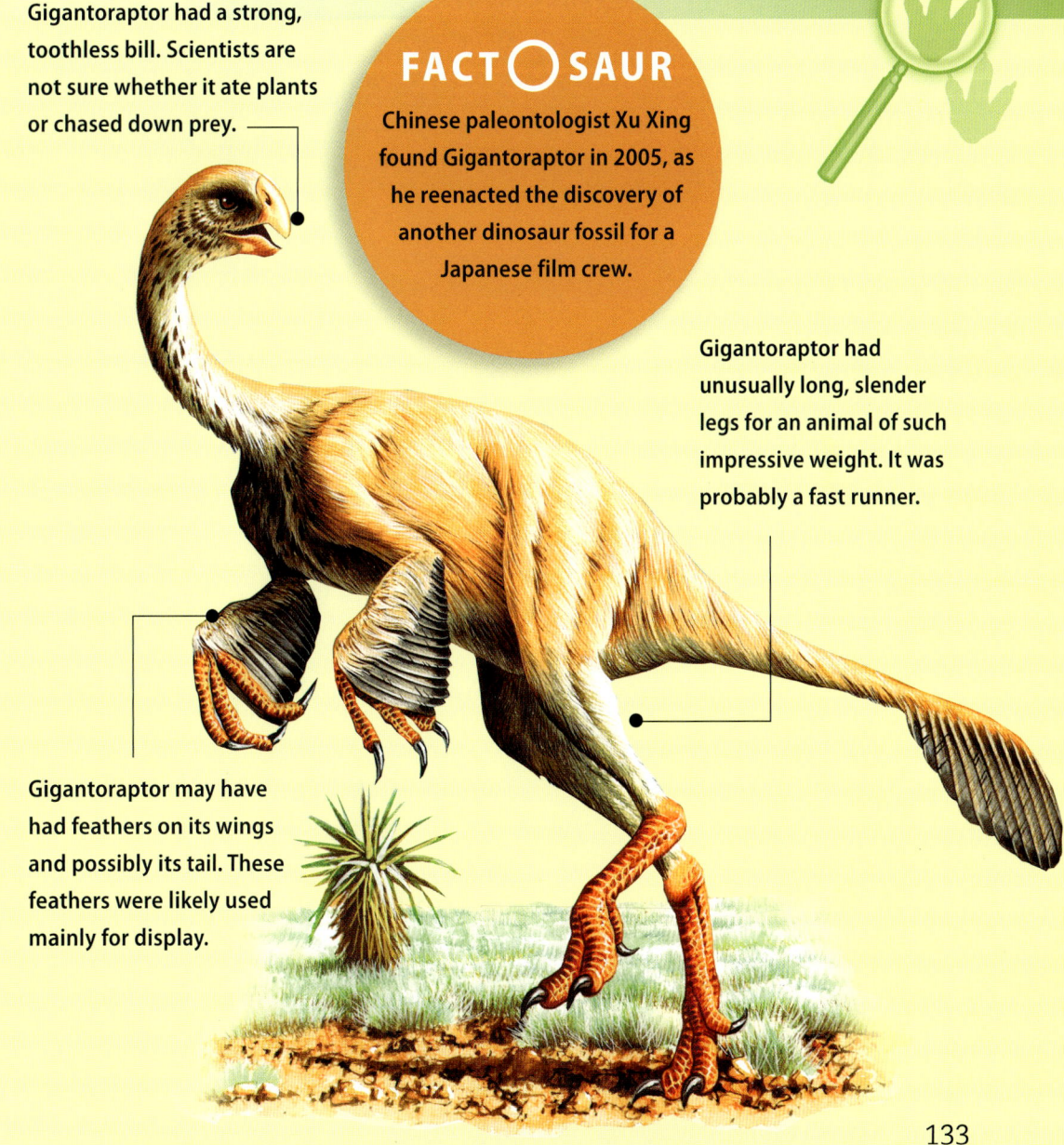

UP CLOSE

Gigantoraptor had a strong, toothless bill. Scientists are not sure whether it ate plants or chased down prey.

FACT O SAUR

Chinese paleontologist Xu Xing found Gigantoraptor in 2005, as he reenacted the discovery of another dinosaur fossil for a Japanese film crew.

Gigantoraptor had unusually long, slender legs for an animal of such impressive weight. It was probably a fast runner.

Gigantoraptor may have had feathers on its wings and possibly its tail. These feathers were likely used mainly for display.

Saurornithoides

(SAWR-or-NITH-oy-dees)
Saurornithoides was a close relative of Troodon and was similar in most ways, though it lived in what is now Asia rather than what is now North America.

FUN FACT

Struthiomimus lived in what is now Canada and had to tolerate cool winters, though at that time, temperatures did not fall as low as they do today.

Struthiomimus

(STROOTH-ee-o-MIME-us)
Struthiomimus ran quickly on its long legs, holding its tail out for balance. It probably relied on speed to escape tyrannosaurs and other predators.

Troodon (TROH-oh-don)

was a birdlike theropod that lived in what is now North America about 70 million years ago. Troodon had a large brain and was probably one of the most intelligent dinosaurs. The name Troodon means "wounding tooth," a reference to the dinosaur's 120 saw-edged teeth, which could cut through the toughest skin.

UP CLOSE

FACT O SAUR

Troodon laid up to two dozen eggs in a nest dug in the ground. Parents guarded the eggs and kept them warm, much as birds do today.

A long, whiplike tail provided balance when Troodon was running.

Troodon had large eyes that faced forward, suggesting it relied on keen eyesight to hunt. It could likely see well in low light and may have even hunted at night.

Strong hind legs allowed Troodon to chase down small prey. These dinosaurs may have hunted in packs.

UP CLOSE

Mononykus (mo-NON-i-kus)

was a birdlike theropod. It was tiny, less than 3 feet (0.9 meter) long, and weighed less than 6 pounds (2.7 kilograms). Unlike most other theropods, Mononykus had only one digit on its hands. It lived in what is now Mongolia about 67 million years ago.

FACT O SAUR

Mononykus had the shortest arms of any known dinosaur. Unlike other theropods, it had only one visible claw on each hand.

Mononykus was likely covered in simple feathers, which may have helped it to stay warm. Scientists do not actually know the color of its feathers.

Mononykus had a birdlike head with a toothless bill, and large eyes to spot the fast-moving insects it ate.

The arms were short but powerful. Each ended in a single banana-shaped claw. Mononykus may have used its claws for ripping into termite nests. It might then have slurped up the insects with its tongue.

Dromiceiomimus
(DROH-mee-see-uh-MIME-us)
Dromiceiomimus was a close relative of Struthiomimus. Its light body and long, powerful legs enabled it to run quicky.

Noasaurus
(NOH-ah-SAWR-us)
Noasaurus was a swift predator that may have hunted in packs. The long claws found with a fossilized skeleton may have grown on the hands rather than the feet.

Elmisaurus
(ELM-ee-SAWR-us)
Elmisaurus was another slender, ostrichlike theropod that relied on speed and its sharp claws to catch prey.

DINO BITE

The Origin of Feathers

Feathers rank among nature's great innovations. Feathers keep such songbirds as cardinals warm even in deep winter, when temperatures plunge far below freezing. Feathers almost never break in flight, even among falcons that dive at speeds of more than 200 miles (320 kilometers) per hour. Feathers can also be beautiful, such as the brilliant feathers the peacock uses to attract mates.

For many years, scientists thought feathers were unique to birds, but a series of remarkable discoveries has shown that feathers first appeared among dinosaurs.

Feathers are rarely preserved in fossils. It was only in 1996 that *paleontologists* (scientists who study prehistoric life) found proof that a dinosaur had feathers. A 125-million-year-old fossil preserved the skeleton of a small theropod dinosaur named Sinosauropteryx. The fossil also preserved traces of feathers. The claim that a dinosaur had feathers was controversial. Eventually, additional fossil discoveries convinced most paleontologists that many theropod dinosaurs had feathers.

Feathers may have originated among small theropods in the Jurassic Period. Some scientists believe feathers appeared even earlier. The earliest feathers were probably bundles of simple strands, like down. These short, fuzzy feathers were not useful for flight. Instead, feathers may have provided insulation, or they may have been important for courtship or other displays.

Some dinosaurs developed larger and more complex feathers. These feathers had a stiff central shaft lined with many strands. These feathers were not as sophisticated as modern flight feathers, but they would have enabled dinosaurs to glide between trees. Many scientists think birds descended from such a feathered dinosaur. Birds became better fliers over time, as both their feathers and bodies became adapted to flight.

Throughout the late Jurassic and the Cretaceous periods, birds and feathered dinosaurs lived side by side. Sinosaur-opteryx had only simple, downy feathers. Yet it lived long after Anchiornis, a birdlike theropod with crude flight feathers that lived about 160 million years ago. Because Anchiornis had more complex feathers, paleontologists believe feathers must have originated even earlier, among dinosaurs that remain unknown to science.

The Ruppell's vulture *(above)* relies on downy feathers to keep it warm. Its flight feathers enable the vulture to soar high above the ground for hours at a time.

New research methods also have played a role in understanding feathers. In 2010, scientists reconstructed the color of some dinosaur feathers by examining them with a powerful microscope. The microscope revealed complex arrays of *melanosomes* (muh-LAN-oh-sohmz—tiny pigment-bearing structures in cells). Melanosomes give modern bird feathers much of their color. By comparing the arrangement of melanosomes in dinosaur feathers with those of modern birds, scientists were able to know their color. Thus, we know that Anchiornis had mainly gray feathers, with black-and-white feathers on the limbs. Sinosauropteryx had mainly reddish and white feathers, with stripes down its back.

Paleontologists continue to search for fossils of feathered dinosaurs and prehistoric birds. Each new discovery brings us closer to understanding the origin of both feathers and birds.

The Rise of Birds

The first known feathered theropods appeared in the Jurassic Period. Some of these dinosaurs almost certainly lived in the trees. They likely used their feathers and winglike limbs to glide between trees, both to feed and to escape predators. Birds are thought to descend from one of these feathered, tree-dwelling dinosaurs.

The precise origin of birds remains unknown, but they probably appeared more than 160 million years ago. Scientists still debate the classification of the earliest feathered theropods. It is not always clear whether these animals were birds or very close relatives of birds. Some scientists even argue that Archaeopteryx, the most famous early bird, may actually have been a small, feathered dinosaur rather than a true bird.

Birds flourished throughout the Cretaceous Period. They became much more diverse, adapting to a variety of environments. There were large diving birds that fed on fish, eaglelike birds that hunted small animals, and small birds that ate only plants. Many birds of the Cretaceous Period were unlike any modern bird, having claws on their wings, a bony tail, and a bill filled with sharp teeth. Others probably looked much like the birds we see today.

Confuciusornis had claws on its wings *(opposite),* **like many other birds from the Age of Dinosaurs. Scientists have found thousands of fossils of Confuciusornis** *(below).*

Anchiornis
(AN-kee-AWR-nihs)
Anchiornis had crude flight feathers on both its long forelimbs and hindlimbs. Scientists have reconstructed the color of these feathers through the study of *melanosomes*. Anchiornis lived about 160 million years ago.

Epidexipteryx
(EHP-ee-dehks-IHP-tuhr-ihks)
Epidexipteryx had four long feathers on its tail. These were mainly used for display, though they also may have provided balance in the trees. The long fingers may have helped it to catch insect grubs.

Xiaotingia
(show-TIHNG-jyah)
Xiaotingia was a very early bird or a closely related dinosaur. It resembled Archaeopteryx in most respects but appeared earlier, about 160 million years ago.

Archaeopteryx (AHR-kee-OP-tuhr-ihks)

is the most famous bird from the Age of Dinosaurs, though some scientists think it was a closely related dinosaur rather than a true bird. This crow-sized animal likely spent much of its time in the trees. It lived in what is now Europe about 150 million years ago.

UP CLOSE

FACT-O-SAUR

Archaeopteryx was discovered in 1861. Its mix of bird and reptile traits provided support for Charles Darwin's new theory of evolution.

Archaeopteryx had sharp claws on its wings. Its strong flight feathers enabled it to glide between trees or possibly even fly. However, Archaeopteryx would not have been a strong flier.

The bill was lined with sharp teeth. Some scientists think Archaeopteryx may have fed on small pterosaurs.

Archaeopteryx had the long, bony tail of a theropod, but the tail was covered in flight feathers.

143

UP CLOSE

Microraptor (MY-kroh-RAP-tuhr)

was a feathered dinosaur that was closely related to birds. The long feathers on Microraptor's limbs would have enabled it to glide between trees or possibly even fly. It lived in what is now Asia about 120 million years ago.

Microraptor had black, shiny feathers, much like those of a crow. It had claws on its forelimbs.

Microraptor was even smaller than Archaeopteryx, growing to only about 2 feet (0.6 meter) long and about 1 foot (0.3 meter) tall.

Scientists continue to debate how Microraptor positioned its limbs in the air. Unlike any animal alive today, it had flight feathers on all four limbs.

FACT O SAUR

One Microraptor fossil appears to have a small bird in its stomach. Microraptor may have snatched birds from the trees or possibly even in midair.

144

FUN FACT

Some scientists have argued that Sinornithosaurus may have had a venomous bite, like many modern snakes.

Shanweiniao
(SAN-way-NYOW)
Shanweiniao was a bird that lived about 120 million years ago. It had fan-shaped tail feathers for improved flight, much like those of a modern bird. However, it belonged to a different group of birds, with no living descendants.

Sinornithosaurus
(SYN-uhr-nihth-oh-SAWR-uhs)
Sinornithosaurus was similar to Microraptor in size and way of life. Beautifully preserved fossils suggest it had striking reddish coloration. It lived in what is now Asia more than 120 million years ago.

FUN FACT

Many Confuciusornis fossils lack the long wirelike feathers on the tail. These feathers may have grown only on males, to attract mates.

Confuciusornis
(kuhn-FYOO-shuhs-AWR-nihs)
Confuciusornis lacked teeth but had claws on its wings. Scientists have found thousands of its fossils because it was one of the most common birds 125 million years ago.

Hesperornis
(HES-per-OR-nis)
Hesperornis was a flightless diving bird that grew to about 6 feet (1.8 meters) long. It lived about 80 million years ago.

Enantiornis (ehn-an-tee-AWR-nihs)

resembled a turkey vulture in many respects, though it had teeth and claws on its wings. The wings reached about 4 feet (1.2 meters) across, making Enantiornis larger than most other birds from the Age of Dinosaurs. Enantiornis lived about 70 million years ago in what is now South America.

UP CLOSE

Like other prehistoric birds, Enantiornis had claws on its wings. But changes in its skeleton allowed it to fly with more agility, power, and efficiency than Confuciusornis and other earlier birds.

FACT O SAUR

Enantiornis belonged to the most diverse group of birds in the Cretaceous Period. All members of this group died out at the end of the Age of Dinosaurs.

Enantiornis had sharp teeth in its bill. It may have been a scavenger that fed on animal r*emains* (dead bodies). It may even have lived like a hawk, seizing small prey in its talons.

DINO BITE

Why Did Birds Survive?

Life on Earth suffered a *catastrophe* (horrible event) about 66 million years ago. Scientists have found strong evidence that an asteroid up to 6 miles (10 kilometers) wide struck in the area of present-day Mexico. The impact threw billions of tons of dust and *debris* (small rocks and such) into the atmosphere, darkening the skies for months and causing temperatures to sharply fall worldwide. Massive volcanic eruptions in present-day India added to the chaos. This turmoil caused many kinds of animals and plants to die out over a short period, an event called a *mass extinction*. Most famously, all the dinosaurs became extinct, except for certain types of birds. Scientists are not certain why those birds survived, while similar kinds of dinosaurs disappeared.

Birds had several traits that may have contributed to their survival. Nearly all of Earth's large animals died in the mass extinction, whether they were dinosaurs or other kinds of animals. Small animals, including birds, generally fared better. The feathers of birds could have kept them warm through the long, dark winter caused by the asteroid strike. In addition, many birds likely fed on seeds, decaying plant matter, or insects, which could have sustained them until conditions improved and plants began to recover. Birds also may have been able to fly away from areas of devastation, to warmer regions that still had food.

The mystery is that many other animals with similar advantages did not survive. Many small, feathered dinosaurs were like birds in most respects. They had feathers for warmth, and some could glide or possibly even fly. Many of these dinosaurs likely fed on foods similar to those eaten by birds. Scientists do not know why none of these dinosaurs survived.

In fact, most birds did not survive the great catastrophe. Many kinds of birds that flourished in the Cretaceous Period died out with the dinosaurs.

Scientists are not certain which groups of modern birds lived before the mass extinction. Some think several groups of modern birds had already appeared by the Late Cretaceous Period, including water fowl and certain flightless birds. Others think only a single group of birds survived the extinction. According to this view, the many kinds of birds alive today arose from this one group of survivors.

The cassowary *(above)* of New Guinea belongs to an ancient group of birds. Scientists do not know why certain birds survived the mass extinction that ended the Age of Dinosaurs.

For the animals that did survive, the extinction created profound opportunities. Both birds and mammals quickly *diversified* (become different from earlier types) and spread around the world. Mammals became the largest animals in most environments, taking on roles previously held by dinosaurs.

For the most part, birds thrived by being small. Perching birds are the most diverse group of modern birds, making up more than half of living bird species. Incredibly, many perching birds weigh less than 1 ounce (28 grams).

The dinosaurs ruled as giants, but their large size helped drive them to extinction. Most birds survive by being small and quick. The journey from mighty Tyrannosaurus to the delicate songbirds that thrive today is a triumph of adaptation, endurance, and good fortune.

Where to Find Dinosaurs

Museums in the United States

ARIZONA

The Arizona Museum of Natural History
53 N. Macdonald
Mesa, Arizona 85201

Theropods, sauropods, and other dinosaurs rule at Dinosaur Hall. Visitors can also explore prehistoric Arizona in the Walk Through Time exhibit.

CALIFORNIA

Natural History Museum of Los Angeles County
900 Exposition Boulevard
Los Angeles, California 90007

After you explore the fossils and skeletons in Dinosaur Hall, get a behind-the-scenes look at how the exhibits are made in the Dino Lab.

University of California Museum of Paleontology
1101 Valley Life Sciences Building
Berkeley, California 94720

Many of this museum's exhibits are viewable online as well as in person.

COLORADO

The Denver Museum of Nature & Science
2001 Colorado Boulevard
Denver, Colorado 80205

Dynamic re-creations of ancient environments as well as hands-on fossils tell the story of prehistoric life.

Dinosaur National Monument
4545 Hwy 40, Dinosaur National Monument
Dinosaur, Colorado 81610

The Dinosaur National Monument is located in both Colorado and Utah. Its world-famous Carnegie Dinosaur Quarry, home to nearly 1,500 dinosaur fossils, is on the Utah side.

CONNECTICUT

Dinosaur State Park
400 West Street
Rocky Hill, Connecticut 06067

Here you will find one of the largest dinosaur track sites in North America. Visitors can also explore the Arboretum, which contains more than 250 species of plants—many dating back to prehistoric eras.

The Yale Peabody Museum of Natural History
170 Whitney Avenue
New Haven, Connecticut 06511

Don't miss the Great Hall of Dinosaurs with its famous "Age of Reptiles" mural—one of the largest in the world.

The Natural History Museum of Los Angeles County, Los Angeles, California

The Field Museum, Chicago, Illinois

GEORGIA

The Fernbank Museum of Natural History
767 Clifton Road NE
Atlanta, Georgia 30307

See a Giganotosaurus and other dinosaurs in the Giants of the Mesozoic exhibit.

ILLINOIS

The Chicago Children's Museum at Navy Pier
700 East Grand Avenue
Chicago, Illinois 60611

Kids of all ages can explore a re-creation of an actual dinosaur excavation, including searching for bones in an excavation pit.

The Discovery Center Museum
711 North Main Street
Rockford, Illinois 61103

Visitors will enjoy the simulated dinosaur dig at this children's museum.

The Field Museum
1400 S. Lake Shore Drive
Chicago, Illinois 60605

Chicago's Field Museum is home to Sue, the largest and most complete Tyrannosaurus rex skeleton ever discovered.

INDIANA

The Dinosphere at the Children's Museum of Indianapolis
3000 North Meridian Street
Indianapolis, Indiana 46208

Experience the world of the dinosaurs with family digs, fossil preparation, and sensory exhibits.

MAINE

The Maine Discovery Museum
74 Main Street
Bangor, Maine 04401

Young visitors to this children's museum can explore the world of paleontology at the museum's new Dino Dig exhibit.

MASSACHUSETTS

The Museum of Science, Boston
1 Science Park
Boston, Massachusetts 02114

A 23-foot- (7-meter-) long Triceratops specimen, found in the Dakota Badlands, is just one of the fascinating fossils on display here.

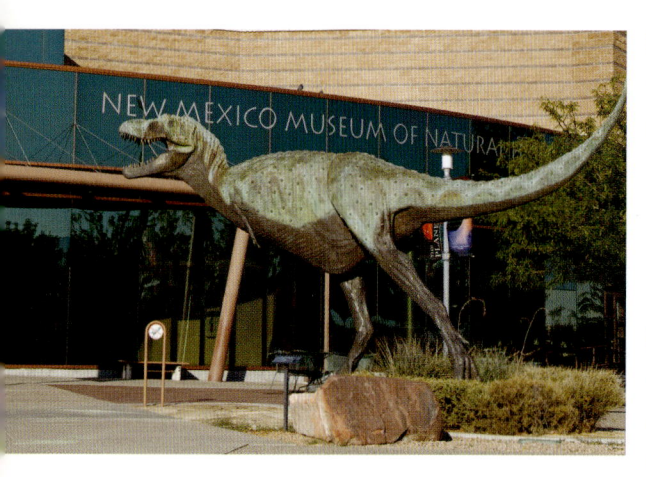

The New Mexico Museum of Natural History, Albuquerque, New Mexico

MICHIGAN

The University of Michigan Museum of Natural History
1109 Geddes Avenue
Ann Arbor, Michigan 48109

Michigan's largest collection of prehistoric specimens lives in the Museum of Natural History's rotunda and galleries.

MINNESOTA

The Science Museum of Minnesota
120 W. Kellogg Boulevard
St. Paul, Minnesota 55102

Do some hands-on fossil exploration at the Paleontology Lab, then get inside the jaws of a giant T. rex to simulate its mighty bite!

MONTANA

The Museum of the Rockies
600 West Kagy Boulevard
Bozeman, Montana 59717

This museum's Siebel Dinosaur Complex houses one of the largest collections of dinosaur fossils in the world.

NEW MEXICO

The New Mexico Museum of Natural History and Science
1801 Mountain Road NW
Albuquerque, New Mexico 87104

The Timetracks exhibit covers the Triassic, Jurassic, and Cretaceous periods.

NEW YORK

The American Museum of Natural History
Central Park West at 79th Street
New York, New York 10024

This museum's famous Fossil and Dinosaur halls house nearly 1 million specimens.

NORTH CAROLINA

North Carolina Museum of Natural Sciences
11 West Jones Street
Raleigh, North Carolina 27601

Home to Willo the Thescalosaurus, an Acrocanthosaurus, and four fossilized whales.

PENNSYLVANIA

The Academy of Natural Sciences of Drexel University
1900 Benjamin Franklin Parkway
Philadelphia, Pennsylvania 19103

Impressive skeletons of massive dinosaurs stalk Drexel's Dinosaur Hall. Visitors can also visit the fossil lab to learn how fossils are prepared and studied.

The Carnegie Museum of Natural History
4400 Forbes Avenue
Pittsburgh, Pennsylvania 15213

The Dinosaurs in Their Time exhibit features scientifically accurate re-creations of environments from the Age of Dinosaurs.

SOUTH DAKOTA

The Children's Museum of South Dakota
521 4th Street
Brookings, South Dakota 57006

Meet Mama and Max, a pair of full-sized animatronic T. rex dinosaurs, and try your hand at a dinosaur dig.

TENNESSEE

The Creative Discovery Museum
321 Chestnut Street
Chattanooga, Tennessee 37402

The Creative Discovery Museum's Excavation Station lets young visitors dig their own dinosaur bones.

TEXAS

The Houston Museum of Natural Science
5555 Hermann Park Drive
Houston, Texas 77030

A world-class Hall of Paleontology includes more than 30 new dinosaurs and many other prehistoric creatures in "action" poses.

UTAH

The Natural History Museum of Utah
301 Wakara Way
Salt Lake City, Utah 84108

The paleontology collections at Utah's Natural History Museum include more than 30,000 specimens.

VIRGINIA

The Virginia Museum of Natural History
21 Starling Avenue
Martinsville, Virginia 24112

Detailed models and interactive features accompany the dinosaur exhibits.

WASHINGTON, D.C.

The National Museum of Natural History—Smithsonian Institution
10th Street & Constitution Avenue NW
Washington, D.C. 20560

Visit the Hall of Paleontology—free of charge—to come face-to-face with dinosaurs, fossil mammals, and fossil plants.

WYOMING

The Wyoming Dinosaur Center
110 Carter Ranch Road
Thermopolis, Wyoming 82443

The combined museum and dig site offers daylong digs for visitors of all ages.

The Carnegie Museum of Natural History, Pittsburgh, Pennsylvania

153

Museums in Canada

ALBERTA

The Royal Tyrrell Museum
1500 North Dinosaur Trail
Drumheller, Alberta T0J 0Y0

Fossil casting allows visitors to make their own fossil replicas at the museum.

ONTARIO

The Canadian Museum of Nature
240 McLeod Street
Ottawa, Ontario, K2P 2R1

Explore the lives—and the eventual extinction—of the dinosaurs in the Fossil Gallery.

The London Children's Museum
21 Wharncliffe Road South
London, Ontario N6J 4G5

The Dinosaur Gallery includes demonstrations, fossil casts, and replicas of many dinosaurs from the Jurassic Period.

The Royal Ontario Museum
100 Queen's Park
Toronto, Ontario M5S 2C6

The dinosaur gallery houses one of the world's best collections.

QUEBEC

The Redpath Museum
859 Sherbrooke Street West
Montreal, Quebec H3A 0C4

Learn about the animals that roamed prehistoric Quebec as well as about many types of dinosaurs.

Museums in the United Kingdom

The Dinosaur Museum
Icen Way, Dorchester
Dorset DT1 1EW,

Highlights include kid-friendly, hands-on computer displays, dinosaur skeletons, and a wide range of fossils.

The National Museum of Scotland
Chambers Street
Edinburgh EH1 1JF,

Allosaurus and Triceratops skeletons are part of a prehistory exhibit, along with dinosaur footprints and a "dino dig" for young visitors.

The Natural History Museum
Cromwell Road, London SW7 5BD

The large dinosaur collection features the first Tyrannosaurus rex fossil ever found, a Baryonyx skeleton, a Triceratops skull, and a famous cast of Diplodocus.

The Natural History Museum, London

Oxford University Museum of Natural History

Parks Road, Oxford OX1 3PW

The outstanding collection of dinosaur fossils and skeletons includes a Camptosaurus, Cetiosaurus, Eustreptospondylus, Iguanodon, Lexovisaurus, Megalosaurus, and a Metriacanthosaurus.

Museums in Australia

The Australian Museum

6 College Street, Sydney
New South Wales 2010

A permanent dinosaur exhibit features high-tech interactive displays; 10 complete dinosaur skeletons, including some native to Australia; and a paleontology lab that is open to young visitors.

The Melbourne Museum

11 Nicholson St., Carlton
Victoria 3053

A kid-friendly Dinosaur Walk exhibition brings the prehistoric world to life with 17 prehistoric skeletons.

The National Dinosaur Museum

Gold Creek Road and Barton Highway
Nicholls, Australian Capital Territory 2913

Home to the largest permanent display of dinosaur and other prehistoric fossils in Australia, including material not on display anywhere else in the world.

The Canterbury Museum, Christchurch, New Zealand

Museums in New Zealand

Canterbury Museum

Christchurch Central, Christchurch 8013

The Geology gallery features fossils and an introduction to the fearsome marine reptiles of New Zealand's prehistory.

Additional Resources

Books

Dinosaur Discovery: Everything You Need to Be a Paleontologist
by Christopher McGowan and Erica Lyn Schmidt (Simon and Schuster Books for Young Readers, 2011)

Activities and experiments show readers how paleontologists examine ancient fossils.

Dinosaur Mountain: Digging into the Jurassic Age
by Deborah Kogan Ray (Frances Foster Books/Farrar, Straus, Giroux, 2010)

Follow fossil expert Earl Douglass on his 1908 hunt for dinosaur bones, which led to the discovery of several amazing skeletons.

Dinosaurs: The Most Complete, Up-to-Date Encyclopedia for Dinosaur Lovers of All Ages
by Thomas R. Holtz and Luis V. Rey (Random House, 2007)

A reference guide to all things dinosaur, from fossil hunting to evolution.

How the Dinosaur Got to the Museum
by Jessie Hartland (Blue Apple Books, 2013)

A dinosaur called Diplodocus is unearthed in Utah and then transported to a dinosaur exhibit at the Smithsonian Museum in Washington, D.C.

The Ultimate Dinopedia: The Most Complete Dinosaur Reference Ever
by Don Lessem (National Geographic, 2010)

This beautifully illustrated and fact-filled dinosaur reference covers almost every dinosaur ever discovered.

DVD's

Bizarre Dinosaurs
(National Geographic, 2009)

Paleontologists lead you on a tour of some of the strangest dinosaurs to ever walk the Earth.

Dinosaur Collection
(Discovery-Gaiam, 2011)

Computer-animated simulations paint a vivid picture of dinosaurs and their world.

Dinosaurs Unearthed
(National Geographic, 2007)

Watch the examination of a mummified dinosaur for a new understanding of how dinosaurs looked, moved, and lived.

Index

A
Abelisaurus, 108
Abrictosaurus, 74
Acrocanthosaurus, 105, 152
Adasaurus, 131
Aeolosaurus, 36
Afrovenator, 98
Age of Dinosaurs, 8-9, 114
   birds in, 143, 149
   ornithischians in, 48-49
   sauropods in, 12
   theropods in, 84, 88, 102, 118
Alamosaurus, 42
Albertosaurus, 111
Alectrosaurus, 108
Alioramus, 112
Allosaurus, 62, 83-85, 93, 100, 154
Alvarezsaurus, 125
Amargasaurus, 37
Ammosaurus, 19
Anchiornis, 139, 142
Anchisaurus, 20
ankylosaurs, 48-57
Ankylosaurus, 47, 57
Anserimimus, 132
Antarctosaurus, 11, 38
Apatosaurus, 27, 31
Archaeopteryx, 116-117, 140, 143, 144
Archaeornithomimus, 132
Argentinosaurus, 39
Armargasaurus, 37
armored dinosaurs.
   See ornithischians
asteroid collision, 44-45, 148
Aublysodon, 111

B
Bagaceratops, 66
Barapasaurus, 24
Baryonyx, 83, 104, 154
Becklespinax, 104
birds, 7, 93
   origin of, 9, 45, 80, 84, 116-119, 138-141
   why they survived, 45, 148-149
   See also theropods
Borogovia, 131
Brachiosaurus, 12-13, 26
Brachyceratops, 66
Brachylophosaurus, 76
Brontosaurus, 27, 31

C
Camarasaurus, 22-23, 31
Camptosaurus, 74, 155
Carcharodontosaurus, 107
Carnotaurus, 109
Carroll, Lewis, 131
cassowaries, 149
Centrosaurus, 68
ceratopsians, 48-49, 64-71
Ceratosaurus, 99
Cetiosaurus, 24, 25, 155
Chasmosaurus, 49, 68
Chialingosaurus, 60
Chiappe, Luis, 115
Chilantaisaurus, 102-103, 107
Chirostenotes, 131
Coelophysis, 90, 94
Coelurus, 122
Coloradisaurus, 16
Compsognathus, 122
Conchoraptor, 128
Confuciusornis, 141, 146, 147

Corythosaurus, 76
Cretaceous Period, 8
   birds and birdlike dinosaurs of, 119, 139, 140, 147, 149
   large theropods of, 85, 98, 102-113
   ornithischians of, 49, 51, 58, 63, 70, 73, 75
   sauropods of, 12, 34-43
Cryolophosaurus, 94

D
Dacentrurus, 62
Darwin, Charles, 143
Daspletosaurus, 82-83
Datousaurus, 27
Deccan Traps, 45
Deinocheirus, 132
Deinonychus, 126
Diatryma, 119
Dilophosaurus, 95
dinosaurs
   bird development from, 9, 45, 80, 84, 116-119, 138-141
   books and media on, 156
   care of young by, 16, 77, 80-81, 129, 135
   extinction of, 44-45, 85, 148-149
   fossils of, 114-115
   in museums, 150-151
   time period of, 8-9
Diplodocus, 10-11, 29, 37
Dracopelta, 52
Dromiceiomimus, 137
Dryosaurus, 74
Dryptosaurus, 110
duckbilled dinosaurs.
   See hadrosaurs

157

E

Edmontonia, 56
Edmontosaurus, 79, 115
egg fossils, 38, 43, 80-81, 117
Einiosaurus, 68
Elmisaurus, 137
Emausaurus, 52
Enantiornis, 147
Eoraptor, 86-88
Epidexipteryx, 142
Erlikosaurus, 126
Euhelopus, 28
Euoplocephalus, 56
Euskelosaurus, 16
Eustreptospondylus, 96, 155
Extinction, 44-45, 85, 119, 148-149

F

feathers
　on birds, 143, 148-149
　on dinosaurs, 93, 117-123, 127, 133, 136, 138-139
fossils, 12, 114-115, 138, 139

G

Gallimimus, 130
Garudimimus, 125
Gasosaurus, 98
Giganotosaurus, 39, 107, 151
Gigantoraptor, 133
Gondwana, 34

H

hadrosaurs, 47-49, 72-79, 81, 115
Hadrosaurus, 76
Harpymimus, 124
Herrerasaurus, 89

Hesperornis, 146
Huayangosaurus, 60
Hylaeosaurus, 52
Hypacrosaurus, 79
Hypselosaurus, 38

I

Iguanodon, 73, 75, 155

J

Jobaria, 34
Jurassic Park (film), 95, 127
Jurassic Period, 8
　ornithischians of, 51, 58, 63
　sauropods of, 12, 22-33
　theropods of, 12, 14, 92-101, 138-140

K

Kaijangosaurus, 98
Kentrosaurus, 62
Kotasaurus, 24

L

Lambeosaurus, 79
Lapparentosaurus, 28
Leptoceratops, 70
Lexovisaurus, 60
Lilienstern, H. R. von, 91
Liliensternus, 91
Lufengosaurus, 21

M

Magyarosaurus, 40
Maiasaura, 77, 81
mammals, 9, 84, 149
Mantell, Mary Ann, 75
Megalosaurus, 97, 98, 155
Megapnosaurus, 94
Melanorosaurus, 16
melanosomes, 139
Mesozoic Era. *See* Age of Dinosaurs

Metriacanthosaurus, 101, 155
Microraptor, 117, 144, 145
Minmi, 54
Mononykus, 136
Montanoceratops, 70
mummified fossils, 115
museums, 150-155
Mussaurus, 18

N

Nanotyrannus, 112
Nanshiungosaurus, 126, 128
Nemegtosaurus, 40
Neuquensaurus, 41
Noasaurus, 137
Nodosaurus, 54
Novas, Fernando, 11

O

Omeisaurus, 32
Opisthocoelicaudia, 41
ornithischians, 7, 46-79
　see also ankylosaurs; ceratopsians; hadrosaurs; stegosaurs
Ornitholestes, 122
Oviraptor, 80, 81, 117, 129, 131, 133
Owen, Sir Richard, 53

P

Pachycephalosaurus, 69
paleontologists, 80, 114, 138, 139
Pangaea, 8, 9, 48, 84, 118
Panoplosaurus, 56
Parasaurolophus, 46-47, 78
Patagosaurus, 24
Pelicanimimus, 124

Pelorosaurus, 34-36
Pentaceratops, 69
Piatnitzkysaurus, 97
Plateosaurus, 17
plesiosaurs, 9, 48, 84, 118
Polacanthus, 54
Proceratosaurus, 94
prosauropods, 12, 14-21
Protoceratops, 67, 80, 115
Protoceratopsians, 64
Psittacosaurus, 64, 66
pterosaurs, 9, 84, 118

Q
Quaesitosaurus, 41

R
Rapetosaurus, 42
Riojasaurus, 17

S
Saichania, 55
Saltasaurus, 43
Saltopus, 90
sauropodomorphs, 12
sauropods, 7, 10-13, 80-81, 102
    Cretaceous, 34-43
    extinction of, 45
    Jurassic, 22-33
    See also prosauropods
Saurornithoides, 134
Scelidosaurus, 53
sedimentary rock, 114
Seismosaurus, 32
Shanweiniao, 145
Shunosaurus, 30
Sinornithosaurus, 145
Sinosauropteryx, 120, 123, 138, 139
skin impressions, 36, 47, 115

Spinosaurus, 106
Staurikosaurus, 89
stegosaurs, 48-49, 58-63
Stegosaurus, 61, 63, 83
Struthiomimus, 134, 137
Struthiosaurus, 55
Styracosaurus, 69
Suchomimus, 104
Supersaurus, 32-33
Szechuanosaurus, 101

T
Talarurus, 55
Tarbosaurus, 112
tectonic plates, 8, 9
Thecodontosaurus, 19
therizinosaurs, 128
Therizinosaurus, 128
theropods, 7
    large, 82-115
    small or birdlike, 116-140
titanosaurs, 34, 43
Triassic Period, 8, 12, 14, 86-91
Triceratops, 64, 71, 151, 154
Troodon, 134, 135
tyrannosaurs, 102
Tyrannosaurus, 7, 84, 85, 103, 113, 149
    battles with other dinosaurs, 47, 57, 64
    dinosaurs related to, 108, 111, 112
    in museums, 151, 153, 154

U
Ultrasaurus, 33
Utahraptor, 124

V
Velociraptor, 67, 121, 127, 131
volcanoes, 45, 148
Vulcanodon, 25
vulture, Ruppell's, 139

W
warm-blooded animals, 93, 121
Wuerhosaurus, 63

X
Xiaotingia, 142
Xu Xing, 133

Y
Yangchuanosaurus, 92-93, 101
Yunnanosaurus, 20

159